Airy Nothings

Religion and the Flight from Time

Peter Heinegg

University Press of America,® Inc.
Lanham • Boulder • New York • Toronto • Plymouth, UK

Copyright © 2014 by University Press of America,® Inc.
4501 Forbes Boulevard, Suite 200, Lanham, Maryland 20706
UPA Aquisitions Department (301) 459-3366

10 Thornbury Road, Plymouth PL6 7PP, United Kingdom

All rights reserved
Printed in the United States of America
British Library Cataloguing in Publication Information Available

Library of Congress Control Number: 2013951298
ISBN: 978-0-7618-6252-9 (paperback : alk. paper)—ISBN: 978-0-7618-6253-6 (electronic)

Excerpt from *Waiting for Godot*, copyright © 1954 by the Estate of Samuel Beckett. Used by permission of Grove/Atlantic, Inc. Any third party use of this material, outside of this publication, is prohibited.

∞™ The paper used in this publication meets the minimum requirements of American National Standard for Information Sciences Permanence of Paper for Printed Library Materials, ANSI/NISO Z39.48-1992.

for Ava and Stella,

precocious atheists

The reader is invited to direct his mind to a moment of deeply-felt religious experience, as little as possible qualified by other forms of consciousness. Whoever cannot do this, whoever knows no such moments in his experience, is requested to read no further; for it is not easy to discuss questions of religious psychology with one who can recollect the emotions of his adolescence, the discomforts of indigestion, or, say, social feelings, but cannot recall any intrinsically religious feelings. We do not blame such a one, when he tries for himself to advance as far as he can with the help of such principles of explanation as he knows, interpreting Aesthetics in terms of sensuous pleasure, and Religion as a function of the gregarious instinct and social standards, or as something more primitive still. But the artist, who for his part has an intimate personal knowledge of the distinctive element in the aesthetic experience, will decline his theories with thanks, and the religious man will reject them even more uncompromisingly.

—Rudolf Otto, *The Idea of the Holy* (1917), tr. John W. Harvey

Contents

Acknowledgments ix

Introduction: Fear of Flowing 1

1 Holy Time 9
2 Holy Space 21
3 Holy God 33
4 Holy People 45
5 Holy Hero Worship 55
6 Holy Books 67
7 Holy Laws 81
8 Holy Afterlife 93

Conclusion: The Triumph of Time 101

Acknowledgments

Thanks to Penguin Books for permission to quote from N.J. Dawood's translation of the Koran and to Grove Atlantic for permission to quote from *Waiting for Godot*. All quotations from the Bible, unless otherwise indicated, are from the King James Version. All other translations, unless otherwise indicated, are by the author.

Introduction

Fear of Flowing

Heraclitus says somewhere that all things flow, and nothing stands still. And he compares existing things to the stream of a river, noting that you couldn't step in the same river twice.

—Plato, *Cratylus* 402a

And some say, it's not that some things move and others don't. Rather, all things are always in motion, but this escapes our notice.

—Aristotle, *Physic* θ3, 253b9

The permanence of change is, to say the least, unsettling. That all things flow, that times change and we change in and with them, is something we admit, but seldom perceive, except in intermittent flashes. Most change is too slow (tectonic shifts), too fast (bullets, light), too vast (the expanding universe), or too minute (the dance of the atoms) to be viewed with the naked eye. Absent time-lapse photography, we can't see our hair or nails or the grass growing, much less the mountains crumbling or the glaciers melting. Of course, when it does come home to us, it often packs a wallop—just ask Rip Van Winkle or Marcel Proust.

Then again, taking in much more than we do, having to process more than a tiny sliver of the data bombarding us from our constantly changing environment, would only cause paralysis. Humans (people driving to work, say) and other animals (lions chasing impala, impala fleeing lions) have to focus on a fraction—and the right fraction—of the signals available—or else.

But, limited as we are, we still make out countless changes, some cyclical, some linear; some major, some minor; some welcome, some not, till eventually it dawns on us that there's nothing we can hold onto for good, not even, and most especially, our own life. And in case this happens to slip your mind, the poets, the storytellers and even the preachers (for their own propagandist purposes) won't fail to remind us. As Pozzo cries out in *Waiting for Godot*:

> POZZO: (*suddenly furious*). Have you not done tormenting me with your accursed time! It's abominable! When! When! One day, is that not enough for you, one day he went dumb, one day I went blind, one day we'll go deaf, one day we were born, one day we shall die, the same day, the same second, is that not enough for you? (*Calmer.*) They give birth astride of a grave, the light gleams an instant, then it's night once more, (*He jerks the rope.*) On!

What to do? Classic responses—other than booze and assorted drugs—include remembering and picture-taking (repeat as needed), reshaping, improving, and "immortalizing" the past, building monuments, painting and sculpting images of the dead, photographing and recording them, giving their names to newborns, etc. But the oldest and most popular strategy is to take refuge in the imaginary world of religion, where all the deficiencies of life, the here-today-gone-tomorrowness of everything, can, they say, be transformed and overcome. As opposed to the evanescence and chaos of earthly time (one damn thing after another), we have the luminous Eternal Now of sacred time. As opposed to the olive-drab, run-down, dingy public spaces we usually inhabit and negotiate, we have the warm radiance of sacred space—holy lands, holy cities, holy shrines, pulsating with *mana* (as nature did, before we ruined most of it). As opposed to infuriatingly imperfect humans, we have the Holy God and Supreme Being (*Kadosh! Kadosh! Kadosh! Hagios! Hagios! Hagios! Sanctus! Sanctus! Sanctus!*), an erratic brain wave, destined to be hysterically amplified down through the ages by prophets and theologians. As opposed to the ragtag mob of hapless individuals flooding the planet, we have a holy, divinely favored people, *our* people—although no particular nation has ever been noted for holy behavior—and, as opposed to filthy, stinking sinners, we have clean-as-a-whistle saints. As opposed to the fallible, fleeting scribbles, inscriptions, and tomes, the messy truckfuls of which are collected and labeled literature, we have the sacred texts of God's Own Word. As opposed to the shifting, contradictory, often cruel mazes of human law, we have the flawless justice—could we but abide by it—of Holy Law. Finally, as opposed to our perpetually fading, perishing selves in an entropic world, we have the blissful dream of an immutable Afterlife, in an eternal heaven, as choreographed, for example, by that holy hallucinator, St. John "the Divine" (Rev. 21.1: "And I saw a new heaven and a new earth, for the first heaven and the first earth were passed away, and there was no more sea," etc.)

Constructing this theological Disneyland wasn't a conscious process, any more than believers ever consciously and expressly take the logical leap that Freud cites as the key to religious faith *The Future of An Illusion*: "When the growing individual finds that he is destined to remain a child forever, that he can never do without protection against strange superior powers, he lends those powers the features belonging to the figure of his father; he creates for himself the gods whom he dreads, whom he seeks to propitiate, and whom he nevertheless entrusts with his own protection" (tr. James Strachey).

But, whatever the origin of religion—Statius' proto-Freudian claim that fear first created the gods still sounds right—there's no doubt that it functions as an opiate, an anodyne for the stresses and strains, the pressures and pains, the slings and arrows of existence-in-flux. But God bless opiates! The only problem is that *this* time-honored, culturally reinforced painkiller is based on a series of delusions and lies. And in the long run, if not sooner, lies, like any set of wrong directions, don't get you where you want to go.

Or is "lies" too strong a word? Didn't Emile Durkheim, a forthright atheist, write, in *The Elementary Forms of Religious Life* (1912), that, "A human institution cannot rest upon an error and lie, without which it cannot exist. If it were not founded in the nature of things, it would have encountered in the facts a resistance over which it never would have triumphed" (tr. J.W. Swain). So there must be *some* truth in religion. But what Durkheim meant is that religion serves as a workable way for a community to affirm itself and bind its adherents together into a "church"; not that its assertions provide an accurate map of the real world. Religion is more like Saul Steinberg's "The World as Seen from Ninth Avenue," Ninth Avenue in this case being the streets of Jerusalem, Rome, Mecca, Salt Lake City, etc.—a flattering, parochial perspective. Religion works pragmatically: like any other cultural product, it can't survive if it doesn't "sell." And it won't sell unless it does do something for its purchasers, which of course it does—providing comfort, consolation, guidance, answers, joyous occasions, etc.—or so they claim.

All those claims, however, are based on various kinds of untruth, which I hope to shed a little light on. But, of course, mistakes can sometimes be fruitful (and believers' most pressing concern is seldom with truth, in any finicky strict sense). In fact, as Nietzsche said, "The falseness of a judgment is to us not necessarily an objection to a judgment [...] The question is to what extent it is life-advancing, life-preserving, species-preserving, perhaps even species-breeding; and our fundamental tendency is to assert that the falsest judgments ... are the most indispensable to us" (*Beyond Good and Evil* 4). Back in the 15th century thinking you could sail more or less directly west from Spain to the Indies was exposed as an error, but it proved to be a very lucrative one, at least for some people. One can choose the wrong spouse, yet have excellent children. So perhaps religion is one of those inspired mistakes (recall the indignant, condescending tone of liberal apologists for faith when they say, "But it's not meant *literally!*") that you just have to play along with in order to savor and profit from.

Unfortunately, once it strikes you that you're operating under false pretenses, how can you go through the religious motions, much less linger in toasty *Schwärmerei*? As a child, one naturally picks up the passions and predilections of one's elders, including an awestruck posture in the presence of what other people call "holy." With reassuring predictability, not only do Jewish, Christian, and Muslim babies grow up to be Jewish, Christian, and Muslim adults; but children wind up adopting the many arcane doctrinal differences that separate, say, Haredim and Reformed Jews, Catholics and Baptists, Sunnis and Shias. Not until later in life, if ever, do some of them discover how little substance there is to their crazy sectarian creeds. But *are* the false judgments of religion, which this book will tot up, "life-advancing"? Does it enhance life to follow God's command to Moses to stone people for gathering sticks on the Sabbath (Num. 15,35), or Jesus' command not to resist evil (Mt. 5. 39) or Muhammad's command (5:33) to crucify his enemies?

And once you realize that Scripture is full of terrible ideas, then what? Remember moss-backed G.K. Chesterton's remark that Times Square at night would be ever so beautiful as long as you couldn't read. But once you've learned to read, you can't pretend you can't. One of the best ways to "lose" your religion is to spend time seriously studying it.

Still, what about those uproarious dancing Hassidim, those beaming Christmas choristers, those serenely long-lived churchgoers, those blissful Muslims on the hajj? And what about the artistic splendors of religion, from the poetry of Isaiah to the cathedrals of France to the mosques of Istanbul and Isfahan (though the number of *modern* religious masterworks is miniscule and diminishing)? Wonderful stuff up to a point, but, whatever the beauty of ancient images, the sublime whisperings or thunderclaps of sacred music, the gorgeous rigmarole of faith, all that has no more necessary cognitive truth or moral value than the older, long cashiered gods and goddesses (cf. the 200 or so cited by H. L. Mencken in his "Memorial Service": Bau, Mulu-hursang, Anu, Beltism Nuskum Ni-zu, Sahi, Aa, Allatu, Abil-Addu, Apsu, Dagan, Elali, Isum, Mamo, Nin-man, Zaraqum Suqamunu, Zagaga, ec.). Ditto for such gorgeous polytheistic playgrounds as the Parthenon, the Pantheon, the Adinath Jain temple in Ranakpur, the Sri Ranganathaswamy temple in Rangam, Teotihuacan, Angkor Wat, etc:—they prove nothing except the talent of their architects and engineers.`

Still, the last word on this should go to Nietzsche, who writes with something like tender regret apropos of *"The Beyond in art"* in *Human, All Too Human* 220 "Not without deep pain does one confess that in soaring to their greatest heights the artists of all times have raised to a state of heavenly transfiguration precisely those ideas that we now realize are false: they are the glorifiers of the religious and philosophical errors of humanity, which they could never have been unless they believed in the absolute truth of those mistakes. Once faith in that sort of truth begins to fall off, the rainbow colors at the limits of human knowledge and imagination will fade away too: so that genre of art can never flourish again which, like the *Divina Commedia*, the paintings of Raphael, the frescoes of Michelangelo, the Gothic cathedrals, takes for granted not just a cosmic but also a metaphysical significance in the objects of art. This will give rise to a moving tale of how there used to be such an art, such an artistic faith." Used to be.

Artists, one might say, pick up whatever symbol systems they find ready to hand and work with them. Nietzsche surely would have been pleased to read Erich Auerbach's magisterial *Dante: Poet of the Secular World* (1929), which shows how earthbound Alighieri was—there's generally a lot less dogma than meets the eye in the Old Masters. Dozens and dozens of Renaissance composers wrote masses based on a secular tune, *L'homme Armé*. Filippo Lippi used his mistress Lucrezia Buti as a model for the Virgin Mary—or was it St. Margaret?

So the lies, or blatant errors, of religion (who knows how much of the deception in the unctuous rumblings of prophets and preachers is deliberate?) aren't erased by their sometimes lovely shape; and the task still remains of tracing the theme of the flight from time through the body of religious belief and practice. Dreams are fine in their place; but we all know the danger of donning a Superman suit and jumping off a tall building. Even imagining such a leap to be possible is, if nothing else, a waste of time.

The ultimate truth about religious experience us that it is a misreading/over-reading of self-generated emotion. Encounters with "the divine" are to encounters with actual others as solo masturbation is to intercourse. The excitement is real enough, but it's self-induced, with the help of old-husbands' tales. (How can it not be grounds for suspicion that nearly all the prophets, visionaries, theologians, ascetical writers, religious founders, and the great majority of saints, mystics, and religious lunatics have been male? Is this some kind of disproportionately male disease, like hemophilia or the echoviruses?)

In any case the rational foundations of religion remain as decrepit and shaky as ever. It's no accident that after sifting through hundreds of pages of testimony by breathless believers in *The Va-*

rieties of Religious Experience (1902), William James, who was ever so eager to join them, could provide no geographic details whatsoever about the terra incognita his subjects said they'd traveled to, however briefly. Their reports showed only one thing for sure, that they had a large subconscious "membrane" that *seemed* to admit signals from some other world. But there was no concrete *there* there, even as no study, however profound or detailed, can ever isolate the supposed transcendental element in holy time, holy places, holy people, holy words, holy books, or holy law, much less find a path to the "Beyond" or its omnipotent, all-loving, immaterial CEO. The whole thing is a category error, like mistaking grammatical gender for biological gender and then discoursing on the masculine charm of second declension Latin nouns (like *fluvius* [river], *lucus* [grove], or *fusus* [spindle])—in other words, pure nonsense.

But, unlike other non-existent beings—rocs, griffons, centaurs or chimeras, King Kong, Medusa, the hydra, or the kraken, moly, ether, the flower of immortality, the philosopher's stone or adamant—God continues to enjoy a huge fan club, an obsequious press, and, outside the pointy-headed set, boundless social respectability. Atheism, whether directed against the Judeo-Christian crowd, Islamists, or Third-World religionists, is seen as cultural arrogance, politically incorrect—and a more or less absolute bar to elected office in the US. Whence the need for an ongoing enfilade of argument, mockery, and contempt, not to change believers' minds—mere philosophy almost never does that—but to make a public case that they can't refute, certainly not with the solemn, hare-brained intoning of "It is my tradition," and perhaps to sow a few slow-maturing seeds of secularism. After all, millions of Americans have been lately turning away from homophobia, capital punishment, and assault rifles, so who knows what crazy idol they might overturn next?

Chapter One

Holy Time

⁸ And thou shalt number seven sabbaths of years unto thee, seven times seven years; and the space of the seven sabbaths of years shall be unto thee forty and nine years. ⁹ Then shalt thou cause the trumpet of the jubilee to sound on the tenth [day] of the seventh month, in the day of atonement shall ye make the trumpet sound throughout all your land. ¹⁰ And ye shall hallow the fiftieth year, and proclaim liberty throughout [all] the land unto all the inhabitants thereof: it shall be a jubilee unto you; and ye shall return every man unto his possession, and ye shall return every man unto his family. ¹¹ A jubilee shall that fiftieth year be unto you: ye shall not sow, neither reap that which groweth of itself in it, nor gather [the grapes] in it of thy vine undressed. ¹² For it [is] the jubilee; it shall be holy unto you: ye shall eat the increase thereof out of the field. ¹³ In the year of this jubilee ye shall return every man unto his possession. ¹⁴ And if thou sell ought unto thy neighbour, or buyest [ought] of thy neighbour's hand, ye shall not oppress one another: ¹⁵ According to the number of years after the jubilee thou shalt buy of thy neighbour, [and] according unto the number of years of the fruits he shall sell unto thee: ¹⁶ According to the multitude of years thou shalt increase the price thereof, and according to the fewness of years thou shalt diminish the price of it: for [according] to the number [of the years] of the fruits doth he sell unto

thee.¹⁷ Ye shall not therefore oppress one another; but thou shalt fear thy God: for I [am] the LORD your God.

—Leviticus 25.8-17

It's the ultimate holiday. The jubilee year—or sabbatical squared—promises pure utopia: no agricultural toil, no more bondage, the reversion of all real estate (except for houses in a walled city) to the original owner, and the end, or suspension, of all "oppression." In his grand farewell address to the Israelites assembled in Moab, Moses told his audience, and all future Bible-believers, that "the word [i.e., the Torah] is very nigh unto thee, in thy mouth and in thy heart, that thou mayest do it" (Dt. 30.13). But this particular mitzvah was quite a stretch; and scripture scholars are agreed that it was never carried out. (How could it be?)

Clearly, it's just a Torah fantasy, of a sort seldom met with in the Old Testament, but on frequent display in the New, especially in the Sermon on the Mount. Still, it illustrates, among other things, the perennial impulse to try to shape and control the irrevocable flow of time. Consider the following religious markers, shaharit (morning prayer), minhah (afternoon prayer), ma'ariv (evening prayer); the canonical "hours" (matins, lauds, prime, terce, sext, none, vespers, and compline); and the five Muslim daily prayers (fajr, dhuhr, asr, maghribh, and isha'a); liturgical seasons: the Days of Awe, Lent, Ramadan, Passover, Easter, Christmas, Eid al-Adh, Ashura. The key to all these times, days, and seasons is that grubby, disorganized, aimlessly plodding, regular time can be, must be, *has been* replaced (temporarily!) by sacred time, which shoots directly toward, and lands smack-dab in the center of, its grand divine goal. Sacred time embodies sacred history (or *Heilsgeschichte*, salvation history), whose landmark events are recaptured and relived in ritual, for example, in the Passover Haggadah, where we read, "In every generation each man should look upon himself [guy-religion] as if he himself came forth out of Egypt. As it is said, And thou shalt show thy son in that day, saying: 'This is done because of that which the LORD did unto me when I came forth out of Egypt'" (Ex.13.8). Ritual bridges the distance from this world to the next, which for Christians and Muslims at least is just around the corner. It's designed to set worshipers free from time by recalling a mythical event that they mysteriously relive. "This is my body," says the priest at the Consecration; "This is my blood."

Thus, the recurrent "Hodie" (today) of the old Roman liturgy, the present always teetering on the edge of eternity, or the Sabbath (God's rest) at the beginning and the end of time. It's a wildly hopeful dream; but view it honestly, and you have to say it crashes. For one thing, all the stories it's based on have evidently been borrowed from somewhere else (the Flood from the Epic of Gilgamesh) or crudely tampered with (the veil of the temple being "rent in twain" at Jesus' death). And since they're all more or less made up, you can't repeat what never happened. The evidence for Moses' having existed is slender, and for the wonders of Exodus, it's zero; but, even granting some minute historical core to the whole business, the fingerprints of the fabulator are everywhere: magical plagues in Egypt? enormous nomadic hordes finding food in a desolate wilderness? God's special favor to Israel shown by repeated annihilation of its enemies? And then, after many non-miraculous centuries (save for the trivial, and non-biblical, miracle of Hannukah) we get … the miracles of Jesus? And Peter and Paul? The myth of the Redemption (who rescued whom from what)? The Trinity? Followed by Muhammad's peremptory tweets from Allah? The Prophet's record-breaking Night Journey (Isra and Mira'j)?

And whatever may have happened in those various Mid-Eastern monotheistic deserts, where revelatory lightning bolts keep hurtling down from heaven, with the passage of time it all grows dimmer, fainter and feebler—like the rest of the past. There are no definitive heroes, no once-and-for-all wisdom, no unchanging reality. Even if he existed, God couldn't undo what's done or bring back what's over. Apart from liturgical play-acting, you can't cross the Red Sea, wander in the wilderness, stand around Mt. Sinai, re-witness the "Savior's" parthenogenetic birth, his multiplication of loaves and fishes, his death and resurrection, or relive the experiences of Abraham, Mary, Muhammad or Hussein. That's why, as the "historical" religions age, new movements, heresies, and sects, often intellectually outlandish ones (Skoptsy, Pentecostalism, Jehovah's Witnesses, Salafism, Mormonism, Christian Science, etc.), can't stop sprouting up, along with new prophets (Joseph Smith, Bahaullah, Mary Baker Eddy, Joseph Kony, and countless other placard-wavers from central-casting): The realm of sacred time ineluctably recedes; and more people find it harder to get there by the well-worn traditional paths. So you need a new gimmick.

But the larger truth is that sacred time itself is a fabrication; so you can't possibly get there or stay there. What people call, and claim to have experienced as, sacred time is simply the encounter of inner sensitivities and expectations with outer stimuli. It's rather like sex: our nervous system is jolted by the right kind of attractants, and the juices flow. You can call this "heavenly, eternal love," if you wish; but that's just a gloss on neurological excitations. There's no separate reality of "Everlasting Love" outside the brains and veins of concrete individual lovers, just as there's no Platonic idea of squirrelness apart from the billions of actual squirrels, living and dead—or any actual realm of sacred time.

The golden haze suffusing believers' Weltanschauung has no reality beyond their own bodies and memories and the forces working on them, as they do on mobs of pilgrims or other worshipers roused by sacred images, hymns, chants, choirs, organs, incense, solemnly intoned catchwords, etc. The most elaborate MRI or detailed dissection will never reveal a soul, and the most exhaustive analysis of the "atmosphere" of a liturgical feast will never produce trace evidence of something "out of this world," because there *is* nothing truly out of this world, just stuff at a greater or lesser distance from the observer. Time is time. *Die Welt is alles was der Fall ist*—the world is what it happens to be, and nothing more: the Wittgensteinian nut that religionists have always cracked their teeth on, and the reason why they switched to a diet of theo-pablum.

But things may be changing. Thanks to the inroads of secularism, belief in, and the supposed experience of, sacred time continues to fade. Just listen to the laughable conservative complaints about the "war against Christmas." Efforts to "put Christ back into Christmas" have long since failed. Christmas is a commercialized potlatch with an (at-best) remote, saccharine-sacred backdrop. And the supreme Christian festivity of Easter has likewise all but disappeared—along with the rest of the liturgical year and for the same reason: the cultural power of religion has been ebbing away in the West since the Middle Ages. The fleshly amusements that have taken its place, from sports to shopping to the high-caloric gorge, aren't necessarily soulful or pretty, quite the contrary; but they've won out because the older feasts fizzled. One can enjoy the athletic liturgical year, shaped by the BCS championship, the Super Bowl, March Madness, Opening Day in MLB, the NBA and NHL finals, Wimbledon and the US Open, the World Series, and the college football season, as much as, or more than, all the threadbare churchy stuff. And the timeless rhythms of nature and the seasons, along with hardy perennials like the calendar year, the school year, the fiscal year, vacations, etc. provide a more believable structuring of time than the imaginary invasion of history by supernatural (but there's nothing "above" nature) folks and forces.

It's true that in Muslim countries Ramadan and Ashura are still going strong; and India is still a religiously drunken land (and, for the most part, religious = backward, despite the cooing multiculturalists). But it seems safe to predict that the spread of literacy, science, the Internet, and so forth will continue to deal devastating blows to the childish naiveté of such beliefs. First of all, sooner or later people learn that their precious tribal and cultural constructs, their festive days and holy seasons, are *not* universal, but local, embarrassingly parochial, and flawed. The Jewish Messiah, the Christian Savior, the Twelfth Imam, et al. mean nothing to the majority of humankind, and rightly so. The possibility that *our* deity, his special messengers and spokesmen, etc. are the only true ones seems increasingly eccentric and self-indulgent. So, to cite one obvious example, our dating systems (e.g., measuring time from the imagined Creation, the birth of Jesus, or Muhammad's Hegira) are one group's quaint idiosyncratic custom, no more valid than any other group's. Each of us has our private circle of special birthdays and anniversaries, centered on ourselves; but we don't expect strangers to pay any attention to them.

There is no intrinsically sacred or God-haunted time, just moments into which we project our personal and communal recollections, longings, expectations, hopes, regrets, etc. The human events, real or imagined or a mix of the two, celebrated in sacred time can never be repeated, recouped, or revived in any definitive sense, for the same reason that you can't step into the same river twice. (Even with all of nature's regular rhythms, no two springs or summers are the same.) Nietzsche's dream of eternal recurrence was a poetic *Gedankenexperiment*, no more. And, because he saw the unstoppable flow of time everywhere, Heraclitus was aptly called the "weeping philosopher."

Look at the changing fortunes of some feast days in our civic religious calendar: Memorial (Decoration) Day morphs from a reminder of Civil War to a celebration of all the War Dead, and—more to the point—the quasi-official beginning of summer, bookended by Labor Day, which signals the end of summer and the start of school, not the lives and struggles of American workers. (The red states hate unions anyway.) Similarly, Armistice Day leaves behind that welcome 11/11/11 moment in 1918 and becomes Veterans Day, for our military "heroes" (thereby ignoring all the noncombatants who suffered and died in our grand and glorious wars, some of them at the hands of those selfsame heroes). And who knows or cares about Flag Day or Arbor Day anymore?

And so it goes. Religious celebrations get watered down and merge with secular romps, as Christmas does with the winter solstice, and Easter with spring fertility rites. Carnival loses its connection with Lent, and becomes just another annual blast. Guy Fawkes Day (or Night) runs out of its original papist-hating fuel, and fades, to be taken over by Halloween, itself one of the best examples of the blending of the sacred and profane (at the rate of one part per thousand). Patriotic memorials diminish too. Bastille Day evokes less enthusiasm with each passing year; and the day will doubtless arrive when another once-unforgettable event from exactly four centuries before that, the Battle of Kosovo (1389), will cease to inflame the nationalist feelings of Serbs.

All time is subjective: as perceived and measured by some human or animal; and since all bodies and groups of bodies are constantly changing in ways that can never be reversed, the contents of our temporal perceptions are forever changing too. It's naïve to objectify our internal sensations the way the Israelites, for instance, do in Joshua 10: 12-14:

> Then spake Joshua to the LORD in the day when the LORD delivered up the Amorites before the children of Israel, and he said in the sight of Israel, Sun, stand thou still upon Gibeon; and thou, Moon, in the valley of Ajalon. And the sun stood still, and the moon stayed, until the people had avenged themselves upon their enemies. Is not this written in the book of Jasher? [And would the book of Jasher bullshit us?] So the sun stood still in the midst of the heaven, and hasted not to go down about a whole day. And there was no day like that before it or after it, that the LORD hearkened unto the voice of a man: for the LORD fought for Israel.

(That's what all the winners, real or fictional, think and say.)

There's sacred time for you! The Master of the Universe arranges a jaw-dropping miracle for his bosom buddies (too bad about the Amorites). Faced with this passage, modern Christian commentators explain with a blush that, of course, the sun didn't *actually* stand still, the Israelites must have simply *felt* as if that day went on forever—always assuming that the battle itself and the ensuing smasheroo victory ever really took place. Not to worry, there have been plenty of actual victories for believers to celebrate: the Battle of the Milvian Bridge, the Battle of the Trench, the Battle of Lepanto, the Mountain Meadows Massacre—oops, forget that one.

Does God take sides and will or effect the slaughter of the losers? Don't ask. Some liberal interpreters like to play it both ways: miraculous events can be read as empirical facts (a smallish band of Hebrew slaves escaped Egypt when an east wind blew over Yam Suph, the sea of reeds; manna was edible deposits by scale insects), but there's no harm in also seeing this as Divine Providence. I mean, come to think of it, isn't *everything* a miracle? And once again we're back in what sacred time is: a feeling of pleasure, a brain-chemical rush prompted by the belief that one is inhabiting, for a while at least, a magic kingdom, i.e., an environment where everything is stacked in our favor. How sweet it is.

But such a world is by definition delusory and infantile. Apart from the fur-lined nest of infancy and childhood—*if* our parents had the resources to build and maintain such a nest—conditions on the planet are generally not so cushy. But people who do live in comfort have a way of extrapolating their coziness way beyond the horizon. Consider Nietzsche's blast against such a complacent perspective in *The Gay Science*, 109:

> *Let us be on our guard!*—Let us be on our guard against thinking that the World is a living being? Whither is it supposed to expand? What is it supposed to feed on? How could it grow and multiply? We do have a rough idea of what the organic is; and

are we supposed to take the unspeakably derivative, late, rare, and accidental features that we perceive only on the surface of the earth, and reinterpret them as something essential, universal, eternal, as do those who call the universe an organism? That disgusts me. Let us be on guard against believing the universe is a machine: it certainly wasn't built with any goal in mind. We do it far too high an honor with the word "machine." ... The astral order in which we live is an exception; this order and the relative permanence that depends upon it have once again made possible the exception of exceptions: the formation of the organic. By contrast, the overall character of the world is, for all eternity, chaos, not in the sense of a lack of necessity, but of a lack of order, structure, form, beauty, wisdom and whatever else we call all our esthetic human qualities. Judged from the standpoint of our reason, the failed throws of the dice are far and away the rule. The exceptions are not the secret goal, and the whole "music box" eternally repeats its tune, which can never be called a melody—and ultimately even the phrase" failed throw" is already an anthropomorphism with an implied reproach. But how could we dare to praise or blame the universe! Let us be on our guard against attributing to it heartlessness or reason or their opposites: it's neither perfect, nor beautiful, nor noble, and has no desire to become any of these things: it's most certainly not striving to imitate humans! It has also no drive for self-preservation—actually it has no drives of any sort. Let us be on our guard against saying that there are laws in nature. There are only necessities: there is no one to command, no one to obey, no one to transgress. If you know that there are no goals, then you know that there is no chance either: for only in the neighborhood of a world of purposes does the word "chance" make sense. Let us be on our guard against saying that death is the opposite of life. The living being is only a species of the dead, and a very rare species at that.

This state of affairs—and can any thoughtful person deny Nietzsche's point here?—strikes many of us as esthetically, intellectually, emotionally, and morally unbearable. Our brains are machines for finding and making order; and pointless necessity makes no sense.

So wish-fulfillment steps in and airbrushes the picture. It ignores the explosion-in-a-spaghetti-factory chaos, concocts various sorts of picturesque imaginary entities (like the constellations), and humanizes everything (the Creator, the "meaning of life," the Last Judgment). It ignores unpleasant, unsettling facts, such as the vast-majority status of the dead (*abiit ad maiores*, said the Romans of their defunct fellows), the long-term futility of life, the "slaughter bench of history," and all the noise and junk floating through the universe (even in our own DNA).

To replace all such depressing data, religion invents the dream of sacred time, a sort of bright red line, expanding into a majestic Camino Real that spans the universe from its cloud-covered godly origins through the frenzies of Doomsday to the glorious *Apokatastasis*, the ultimate tying up of loose ends, reconciliation, repair, and resurrection. It's all perfectly fictitious; but, no matter, its components are so satisfying, e.g., the inexplicable human eavesdropping on God, the spectacular, undeserved gifts he gives (everything from the Holy Land itself to the Blessed Mother's intact hymen), the preternatural prophecies (all of them bogus), the priestly tirades disguised as divine dictation, the whole elaborate fairy tale of the Lord's intervention on behalf of "his" beloved children, that it seems a shame not to go along with it. Regular, garden-variety time is not just a drag; it's an awful dead end. And if the only way to escape it is through desperate falsification, then let 'er rip.

Presto-change-o, by doing this we transform poor human lives, at once preprogrammed and haphazard, into sacred dramas. While it might be hard to apply that to every last specimen of the ragtag human race, it at least holds for exceptional persons like ... *us* (didn't Mr. Rogers, an ordained minister, tell us we were special?). So we have the common carbon of our days on earth transmuted into "immortal diamond": the lost paradise of childhood (the Romantics and the classic novelists taught us all about that), our adolescent beginnings, humble yet pregnant with potential, our unique or serial choices of profession, mate, and community, with—who knows?—some memorable last words in the offing. We learned from Rousseau, among others, that sacred history wasn't limited to the Bible: it's the contents of our here-and-now consciousness. Because, *mutatis mutandis*, we are all so many Isaiahs, Jeremiahs, and Ezekiels living in privileged communion with the Universe (or the Almighty Dad or whomever) and passing on privileged communiqués to others. Democratic theology!

Except things don't work that way. Immediacy doesn't equal sacrality. Yes, our sensorium feels a jolt when someone calls our name, caresses our skin, or seems to respond joyfully to something we say or do. But to label any part of this process "holy" is a leap in the dark. There are lots of ways of getting *frissons* (e.g., from hearing voices or popping pills) and then talking others into getting them too, whence the infectious nature of fads, frauds, phobias, fixations, etc. And religions. But in the final analysis there's nothing in the High Holy Days, Christmastime, or Ramadan, etc. that believers didn't put there first, as surely as they do by wrapping presents, stuffing piñatas or depositing money in the bank. But that doesn't validate an absent-minded thrill upon rediscovering the results of one's own efforts. An echo is not a reply.

Perhaps the clearest example of the fake coincidences and pseudo-rhymings of sacred history can be found in the Christian telling of Jesus' life as the fulfillment of Old Testament prophecies. He was born in the "City of David," Bethlehem (actually in Nazareth). His father was of the house and family of David (but Joseph wasn't Jesus' father.) As an infant he was almost murdered by a Pharaoh-like King Herod. He went down into Egypt as the Hebrews did at the end of Genesis, until, like the Israelites, God called him out of the country. He was tempted in the wilderness, as Israel was, but, unlike Israel, passed all the tests with flying colors. He performed miracles like Elijah and Elisha (fasting spectacularly, raising the dead, walking on water, sailing up into heaven, healing lepers, multiplying meager food supplies, predicting the future, etc.), taught like Moses (on a mountain), spent three days and nights in the tomb as Jonah did in the belly of the whale, and so on.

All of which would have been far more impressive, if it weren't plain that the gospel portrait of Jesus was modeled on the Old Testament, so that, for instance, Jesus *had* to enter Jerusalem in triumph on a donkey *because* Zechariah 9.9 said the Messiah would. Jesus' entire career was a foregone conclusion, because the people who believed in him saw him as the Messiah, as surely as Jews and Muslims have always known *a priori* that everything God revealed to their great men is completely and necessarily true. But such faith is based on rumors, fables, visions, dreams, poetic fantasies, hopeful speculations—in a word, airy nothings.

Chapter Two

Holy Space

And Jacob woke out of his sleep, and he said, "Surely the LORD is in this place, and I knew it not. And he was afraid, and said, "How dreadful is this place? This is no other but the house of God, and this is the gate of heaven."

—Gen. 28.16-17

Among the theists, who reject the use of images, it has been found necessary to restrain the wanderings of the fancy, by directing the eye and the thought toward a *kebla*, or visible point of the horizon. The prophet was at first inclined to gratify the Jews by the choice of Jerusalem; but he soon returned to a more natural partiality; and five times every day the eyes of the nations at Astracan, at Fez, at Delhi are devoutly turned to the holy temple at Mecca.

—Edward Gibbon, *Decline and Fall of the Roman Empire,*
Chapter L

Sacred space has to be the coolest, most user-friendly domain of religion since there's so much of it, so many outstanding (albeit competing) holy tourist sites, such a vast supply of holy *Sehenswürdigkeiten*, as the Germans call them, things-worth-seeing, around the world. True, non-Muslims can't visit Mecca; but they can always go to the Dome of the Rock. Non-Jews are welcome to pray or stare at the sex-segregated Western Wall; and Christian cathedrals, from St. Peter's to Chartres, are open to anyone not immodestly dressed or carrying a suspicious backpack.

Of course, once a sacred shrine is viewed simply as a one-to-three-star Michelin attraction, it ceases to be straightforwardly sacred; and in places where tourists mingle with worshipers, a certain amount of tension is bound to arise—a point brought home to me decades ago when I saw my wife being forcibly escorted from the Imam Reza shrine in Mashhad, Iran: even though she was wearing a chador, her blond hair, Dr. Scholl shoes (and her unbelieving heart, which the guards took for granted) clearly made her an unwanted presence in that great Islamic adytum. Meanwhile, the sighs, sobs, and shouts of the myriad crazy pilgrims in the shrine continued unabated.

But, wait, what gives a wise-ass kaffir the right to call those pilgrims "crazy"? Can the same be said of pilgrims to Czestochowa, Santiago de Compostela, Lourdes, Fatima, and Medjugorje? You bet it can. In a hailstorm, thunderstorm, or volcanic eruption, there are objective hailstones, lightning bolts, torrents of rain, or volcanic ash flying through the air and threatening our heads. But in the case of "spiritual" emanations from sites like the tomb of Imam Reza, whose corpse has been quietly disintegrating since 818, we're dealing with auto-suggestion. The emotions felt in such places are real enough; but their subjective source is all too familiar. When Freddy in *My Fair Lady* sings, "Does enchantment pour out of every door?/ No, it's just on the street where you live," everyone in the audience not similarly besotted with Eliza Doolittle realizes how futile it would be to head to that particular street to capture and taste that promised enchantment.

Generations of guileless pilgrims have been flooded with copious phantasmagoria (scriptural texts, myths, legends, lies), and so are ready to emit, and react to, its stored-up gushes. The shrines and their décor, the primed and conditioned throngs, and the god-laden air almost inevitably prompt a passionate release. Consider *shokeling* Jews or the hymn-singing, weeping masses at revival meetings, Christian glossolalists all over the world, the *penitentes* in Spain and Mexico, the self-crucifiers in the Philippines, the white-robed host of pilgrims on the hajj (many of the women must find that a nice break from their nunnish black uniforms back home), ecstatic Shiite flagellants on Ashura. There's no essential difference between any of them and the shrieking crowds that swarmed around the Beatles, the delirious German mobs in *Triumph of the Will*, or the victory parades and car-burning riots after championship games. Enthusiasm (in the original sense of being possessed by a god) has nothing to do with the truth.

Religion, as Durkheim says, is all about *us*. Full disclosure: the foregoing and any future comments on religious emotion are rooted in, among other things, long years of personal experience. As a tween-and-teenage Catholic in the 1950s I unselfconsciously became a church-junkie. The seductive *Gesamtkunstwerk* of dim lighting, hushed sound, musty air, cool marble pillars, the trace odors of wax and incense smoke, the organist rehearsing in the choir loft, the color patterns traced on pews, walls and floor by stained-glass windows (most of them gauche-to-hideous, but nonetheless kaleidoscopic on sunny days), seldom failed to spark my youthful piety. (In a mild irony, by the time I first traveled to Europe, in my mid-twenties, to see some of the grandest masterpieces of Christian architecture, I had already lost my faith—or my faith had lost me—and could feel esthetic awe but no religious tremors.) In my adolescent post-communion "thanksgiving" I sometimes managed to stir up wavelets of imageless, faintly erotic yearning for the Christ-Out-There. Such throbs were informed and amplified by catechism classes and contact with priests, nuns, and brothers at my parochial school. The key to continuous access to this mystical sphere—I realized in retrospect—was to shield it from the bright light and strong winds outside. Eventually it shone, and they blew, in; and the whole contraption collapsed.

At any rate I see no reason to doubt that some process like my callow reveries—minus the later disillusionment—goes on in the brains of most believers. Of course, non-Episcopalian Protestants and, to a lesser extent, Jews, have to do without the lavish ceremonies of the RCC, but even Catholic worship is a mostly drab affair these days. Actually, *all* modern versions of holy space pale by contrast with the electrifying accounts of it we find in the Bible. No burning bush or Sinai sound-and-light show, for example, has been sighted for millennia. The overwhelming visions of God, in the Temple and elsewhere, that made Isaiah and Jeremiah stutter in fearful rapture are gone, presumably forever. So too the death rays that struck Aaron's sons Nadab and Abihu for offering the wrong kind of incense (Lev. 10.2), and Korah, Dathan, and Abiram for rebelling against Moses (Num. 16), or Ananias and Sapphira (Acts 5) for lying to Peter. *That's* holiness, Rudolf Otto's *mysterium tremendum et fascinans* (we've seen how he pities those who've never felt it.) Of course, episodes like the Flood, the nuking of Sodom and Gomorrah, or the annihilation of the Assyrian army (2 Kings 19.35) must have been still greater spectacles, but the Bible's account of those mega-disasters skips the gory details and so is less powerful than it might be.

As everyone admits, that sort of firepower has vanished—at least in the hands of an angry God. But religion still has its holy sites, again so long as it buffers them from time and the weather. One might be tempted to attribute the generally dulled and dampened modern sense of sacred space to the boring, sterile churches and synagogues built over the last century or so, which compare with the great basilicas of old somewhat as today's suburban banks, all cinder block, linoleum, cheap carpeting, and low-ceilinged-office look, compare with the soaring 19th century Temples of Finance, like the old National City Bank in Manhattan. But the badness or blahness or banality of contemporary sacred places (megachurches! The Crystal Cathedral! Temple Square in Salt Lake City! Our lady of Peace of Yamoussouko, the world's largest church!) likely arises less from architectural ineptitude than from the fact that in these decadent times the sense of the sacred *tout court* has been withering away.

Yet the larger truth here is that all perceptions of sacred space, old and new, like those of sacred time, are self-generated illusions. An uninitiated outsider has to be *told*, like Moses, that he or she is in holy territory—as I myself was told, wordlessly, by a uniformed soldier with a rifle aimed at me some years ago when I attempted to sit down in the courtyard of Anitkabir, Turkey, two hundred yards or so from the mausoleum of Mustafa Kemal in Ankara. *This*, it turned out, was holy ground for patriotic Turks; and woe betide the irreverent infidel who tried to rest his feet in that sacred presence.

But if you blindfolded people and placed them in front of some world-famous sacred monument, they couldn't get the appropriate sacred vibes, so long as they were uncertain whether they were at the Erechtheum, the Western Wall, the Prambanam in central Java, the Virgen de la Pax in Trujillo, Mexico, the statue of Peter the Great in Moscow, the blockbuster giant Christ in Swiebodzin, Poland, or the erotic (non-religious) carvings in Khajuraho, Madhya Pradesh. Objective emanations from ordinary space, e.g., light, heat, smells, liquids, or radioactivity can be scientifically measured. Artistic qualities in natural or architectural space can be rationally analyzed and compared. But mana can't—not least of all because it doesn't objectively exist.

Lincoln got it wrong when he said, "But in a larger sense we cannot dedicate, we cannot consecrate, we cannot hallow this ground. The brave men, living and lead, who struggled here, have consecrated it far above our power to add or detract." The thousands of corpses buried at Gettysburg and the corpses of the ex-combatants later buried elsewhere didn't make the place holy, nor was that anyone's intention before or during the battle. The fact is that a select group of emotionally involved, politically minded individuals got all worked up—and some people continue to get worked up—whilst on or around the battlefield, when they thought or think about the horrific bloodshed that took place there. And *they* "hallowed" it—for themselves. Supporters of the Confederacy probably fail, by and large, to share that sense of edification at Union gravesites. And pacifists may well turn away from the scene in pity and disgust, because in so many ways neither this battle nor the Civil War as a whole was necessary, noble, or, practically speaking, a good thing.

The same problem arises if, dropping any blindfolds, one takes a Sioux adult to Mount Rushmore, a Jew to the massive equestrian monument honoring Bogdan Khmelnitsky, the great 17th century Cossack butcher, in St. Sophia Square, Kiev; a Gandhian to the statue of Genghis Khan (132 feet tall) in Tonjin, Mongolia; or a surviving relative of one of the tens of millions slaughtered by Mao Zedong to the 105-foot-tall statue of the Helmsman in Juzhizhou, China. It's not sacred space to *them*. And, of course, in the same way the secular visitor can walk completely unmoved down the Via Crucis in Jerusalem, through the basilica at Lourdes, or the campy shrine of the North American Martyrs in Auriesville, N.Y.

Which stands to reason, because in the final analysis there is nothing sacred (in the magical sense) at all. Unless they get blown up like the Buddhas of Bamiyan, the titanic statues of the world's great religious and political heroes, the Buddha, Jesus, Lenin, Mao, etc. will ultimately become latter-day versions of Ozymandias, on a par with non-religious monuments like the statue of the Dallas Zoo's Giraffe (67 feet) or the Jolly Green Giant in Blue Earth, Minnesota (55 feet). Eventually, the passionate faith that built them will fade and decay, like all things mortal. (The bigger they come, etc.) Consider the absurd monster statues on Easter Island, once adored by the brainsick natives, and now featured in a Paul Noth cartoon mocking Mitt Romney (where an expert informs a tourist, "They keep watch on the offshore accounts").

All over the planet we find overwhelming evidence of how ordinary time has vanquished sacred space: the ruins of innumerable temples, some of them to gods we can't even identify, show how short the life of divinity is. What was going on at Göbekli Tepe, Turkey apparently the oldest religious structure anywhere (ca. 9,000 BCE)? Who exactly was worshiped at the far more recent Pyramid of the Sun in Teotihuacán, Mexico? The god Taishi, we're told, was venerated in China's Zhongyue Temple, but who was he? What about Stonehenge? The massive and incredibly numerous statues of Sekhmet? (My family has a splendid house cat named Sekhmet.) For ages nobody has worshiped any gods at all in the Temple of Luxor, the ziggurats of Iraq, the Mayan temples of Yucatan, the Valley of the Temples in Agrigento, or the Sanctuary of Asclepius at Pergamon.

Nor is there any reason to find this surprising: religions are human artifacts; and like all artifacts they fall apart. While they may do so slowly and majestically, they can also be wrecked, i.e., deprived of their sacredness, by human aggression. Once you've paved Paradise and put in a parking lot, it's not Paradise anymore. Google the topic "destroyed sanctuaries" (22,900,000 sites as of early 2012), and sample the rich variety of havoc visited on one people's temples, shrines, and holy places by ultra-zealous raiders (often Christian) from another people. And needless to say, the gods whose holy places were captured or wiped out didn't lift a finger to prevent the sacrilegious annihilation: they were already dead.

In a famous religious debate the prophet Elijah mocked the priests of Baal for fruitlessly appealing to their absent or impotent Lord: "Cry aloud: surely he is a god; either he is meditating or he has wandered away [i.e., to relieve himself], or he is on a journey, or perhaps he is asleep and must be awakened" (1 Kings 18.27,

NRSV). A witty thrust, except that Yahweh himself stood by helplessly when the Babylonians sacked his temple in 586 BCE, and the Romans leveled it for good in 70 CE. Sacred space turns out to be as volatile as any other item on the real estate market.

But let's leave aside the dead sacred spaces and look at the all-time, bar-none, as-live-as-they-come exemplar of holy ground: what snotty David Hume calls "the holy temple at Mecca," the Kaaba. "Sacred" often has the connotation of "forbidden" (cf. Arabic *haram*); and the Kaaba is by definition off limits to more than three-quarters of the human race, not to mention the vast majority of Muslims who can't afford to go on the hajj and who couldn't get into Mecca even if they had the funds, since there isn't enough room (fewer than two-tenths of a percent of Muslims worldwide go there in any given year, and some of those are repeat-visitors). Of course, you can watch the Kaaba in comfort on your TV, as I once did at a halal sandwich joint in Marseilles, where they had a live video feed from Mecca running all day (though no one paid any attention to it).

So what is it about the Kaaba that makes the Cube (its literal meaning) so holy? Islamic fairy tales about its being built by Abraham (Ibrahim) and Ishmael (Ismail) over two millennia before the Common Era are palpable nonsense, because there's no evidence that the father and son team, assuming they were historical, ever went there. (And wasn't the son in question Isaac anyway?) Muhammad's claim that the most sacred item inside the Kaaba, the Black Stone (*al Hajar al-Aswad*) was originally flung down to earth by God for Adam and Eve to build an altar with it is patently worthless. The current Kaaba (it has been torn down and reconstructed many time) is a big granite box, roughly 36' by 42' by 43', made with stones quarried nearby. Originally a pagan shrine, it was magically purified by removing the hundred of idols it once contained, and serves both as the Qibla, the focal point for all Muslims praying anywhere on the planet (after a brief, misguided period when Jerusalem served that purpose) and the very best spot on earth for counterclockwise circumambulation, ideally seven times in a row during the hajj.

So where does all its holiness come from, especially now that Abraham and Ishmael's original edifice is long gone? That's sad, but today's pilgrims can always vie to kiss fragments of the Black Stone, which once was kissed by Muhammad himself, and thus are at only one degree of separation from the holiest man who ever lived (never mind his fanatical temper tantrums and only-for-the-boss phallic romps in the Qur'an), or something.

The Kaaba has the huge disadvantage, when compared with, say, the Pantheon, Chartres Cathedral, or the Shah Mosque in Isfahan, of having next to no beauty; but of course that doesn't matter when it comes to sacred space. Are most ziggurats beautiful? Most stupas? Most Mormon temples? Most storefront churches? Holiness is power, and the Kaaba emits power as surely as the Grand Coulee dam emits electricity.

Or does it? Short of an unobtainable test trot around the Kaaba, one can only suspect that all the sacred pulsations in the pilgrims who manage to arrive there are self-generated, released by their internal trip-wires after long years of conditioning. After all, that's what happens to the crowds of well-informed sports fans when they enter *their* sacred spaces, such as Yankee Stadium, Wembley Stadium, the Rose Bowl, Bell Centre (Montreal), or the All England Tennis Club in Wimbledon. And note that in all these grand athletic venues, as with the Kaaba, we're not talking about some sort of virginal, unchanged locale, but of much-modified, redesigned and rebuilt construction sites. To continue the analogy, it's not likely that people with zero interest in baseball, soccer, football, hockey, or tennis would feel more than the faintest stirrings of *das Heilige* upon taking their seats in such world-famous shrines to athleticism.

Worse yet, any reader willing to admit that there are serious parallels between playing fields and praying fields has already crossed an important philosophical line. The comparison itself strongly suggests that secular games and sacred rituals are akin: purely human performances (routines, arrangements, systems), arbitrary from the start and forever open to alteration and innovation (the d.h.!, instant replay!, Hawk-Eye!, new rules from FIFA!). Like sports, religion is all about us. It celebrates us, the participating audience, through the exploits of some of our stellar forebears in a partly familiar, partly alien environment, set up to enhance our feelings of well-being. No wonder St. Paul said, "Athletes exercise self-control in all things; they do it to receive a perishable wreath, but we an imperishable one. So I do not run aimlessly, nor do I box as though beating the air; but I punish my body ...; so that after proclaiming to others I myself should not be disqualified" (1 Cor. 9.25-27, NRSV). The idea seemed so natural that whoever pretended to be Paul in 2 Timothy picked it up and literally ran with it: "I have fought the good fight, I have finished the race, I have kept the faith" (4.7). True, it was foolhardy to dream that holy jocks would one day be crowned by "the Lord, the righteous judge" (who reappears as Grantland Rice's "One Great Scorer"); but the sports metaphor was irresistible—even as it hinted that the religious game fulfilled and exhausted itself in the playing, with no need for an eternity-long wrap-up or rehash. When it's over, it's over.

And so there is no objective sacred space, unless you want to count our dwindling supply of natural wonders. Many people, in fact, would cite America's national parks—take your pick, the Grand Canyon, Yosemite, Mt. Rainier, Zion, the Tetons, whatever—as true "sacred space." And at least some of the travelers or hikers there are touched by powerful sensations, which can at times be summoned up again just by looking at one's photos of old vacation trips.

But the catch is that, absent the human and animals inhabitants of mountains, deserts, forests, sea shores and river banks, etc., there's nobody whatsoever sending messages to any passers-by.

The universe—meaning its more presentable parts, since nobody cares about the 99.999999999999% taken up by empty space or astral "bodies" far too hot or cold to live in—developed the way it did randomly and automatically. Some sections *are* way more beautiful or interesting than the others, but not essentially different from, and absolutely not "holier" than, the others. The universe "means" nothing, despite our devoutly invoking the pathetic fallacy to talk about it for untold millennia: it has, apart from us, no messages, no self-conscious force, no God or Holy One of Ground of Being or Man Upstairs who cares a hoot about us. And human attempts to impersonate him have not worked out well either. Sacred space is, and always has been, an echo chamber.

Chapter Three

Holy God

But who am I, and what is my people, that we should be able to offer so willingly after this sort? For all things come of thee, and of thy own have we given thee. For we are strangers before thee and sojourners, as were all our fathers: our days on the earth are as a shadow, and there is no abiding.

—1 Chronicles 29.141-5

Every good gift and every perfect gift is from above, and cometh down from the Father of lights, with whom is no variableness, neither shadow of turning.

—James 1.17

All right, no holy time, no holy space; but what about the holiest thing anywhere? God is the cure for time and change. Of course, no one has ever met God, except in a few blurry moments of self-induced rapture; and so believers have to turn to the theologians (i.e., God-talkers, almost always male) for information about the Almighty Ghost in the Great Beyond. And the things you can learn from them! First of all, that we mustn't expect to *understand* God, not in the usual sense of understanding at least. *De Deo loquimur*, says Augustine in his 117th sermon, *quid mirum si non comprehen-*

dis? It would be suspicious if we *could* understand "him." Whence Paul's obsessive-compulsive use of the word "mystery" (which comes from a verb meaning "to shut one's eyes—you can't look at divinity too closely).

Like all theologians, from the gentle Philo of Alexandria to the unspeakable Ayatollah Khomeini, Paul writes about an imaginary realm, e.g., "Behold I show you a mystery; we shall not all sleep [i.e., die before the Second Coming of Christ], but we shall all be changed [transformed from mortals into immortals]" (1 Cor. 15). God alone knows what reasons "the Apostle" has for claiming this (Paul claims to have taken one flying visit to Paradise [2 Cor. 12], but, dang, the words he heard there were "unspeakable, which it is not lawful for a man to utter" (v. 4), so we'll never know. God-talkers can come up with lists, like the famous ninety-nine names of Allah, of supposed divine "qualities," from the recondite "aseity" and "Patripassian" to homier ones like "kindness" and "compassion" (though the latter have been conspicuous by their absence).

Since just about everyone, except for a handful of unread process theologians, agrees that God is perfect, it's easy enough to string out the catalog of fabulous, mostly negative adjectives (infinite, invisible, immaterial, immortal, etc.) to "describe" him. On the assumption that, like other absolute monarchs, God enjoys immoderate flattery; theologians have heaped up piles of Very Nice Adjectives to tickle his fancy, notably good, great, holy, and the rest. As David Hume writes in Section VI. Origin of Theism from Polytheism in *The Natural History of Religion* (1757) with his customary acumen:

> In proportion as men's fears or distresses become more urgent, they still invent new strains of adulation and even he who outdoes his predecessors in swelling up the titles of his divinity, is sure to be outdone by his successor in newer and more pompous epithets of praise. Thus they proceed, till at last they arrive at infinity itself, beyond which there is no farther progress. And it

is well, if, in striving to get farther, and to represent a magnificent simplicity, they run not into inexplicable mystery, and destroy the intelligent nature of their deity, on which alone any rational worship or adoration can be founded.

Among God's most useful qualities "unchanging" would have to rank very high. It's true that never in the history of the universe, so far as we can tell, has a*nything* ever not been mutable. And how could supremely changeable mortals ever identify with and grasp immutability or adjust to it in the afterlife? But it sounds terrific; one of those things that sooner or later comes in handy, like Krazy Glue or Drano or duct tape. If God is unchanging, then maybe he can save us from this world of time and change. (Of course, if he's beyond time—whatever that means—how could time-bound creatures like us ever get to him?) But, wait, if God *is* out there, all the human beings who die and disappear, all the hopeful human projects that crash and burn, the whole transitory universe, peopled and otherwise, might not be doomed to oblivion. Whence the ineradicable longing for Saviors, Rescuers, and Redeemers.

Still, how exactly how would God save the day? Not much thought seems to be given to this, except in the various silly scenarios of the afterlife (see Chapter 8, "Holy Afterlife"). But that won't cut it. Among many other things, the nature of the divine savior is completely unknown/invented from the whole cloth. Theologians start out from the axiom that God is a person, because that's the most elaborately organized life form we know. But all the persons *we've* ever seen are a massive assortment of specific features, which necessarily implies a googolplex of negatives (this-but-not-that-s). Therefore in the strict sense, persons are utterly limited beings. But God has no limitations; and so he (she, it, they) can't be a person in any recognizable sense. Such a "godhead," as religionists like to say, wouldn't be anything in particular, except perhaps a baffling conceptual flourish. Whence the vogue for "apophatic" theology.

For convenience' sake, we generally refer to God as "he," because in our culture (all cultures?) "he's" are more powerful than "she's." And, from the traditional sexist standpoint, masculinity is more "neutral," i.e., less overtly sexual, than femininity. Finally, a genderless person simply doesn't compute for us. So, characterizing God as a non-stop stream of things he isn't—gendered, embodied, rooted in anything concrete—doesn't get us very far. And the typical superlatives assigned to God—all-knowing, all-wise, almighty, all-good—fall apart the moment one looks for any evidence of them. A God who knew everything, and possessing a modicum of divine power and human decency, would have to have made a much better world than the disastrous mess we have now.

What's going on here is the old God-of-the-gaps plugging-and-patching, the deity as default solution for otherwise maddening problems. At his essential core, the God of monotheism seems to be defined as a source of scary power (which, when *not* exercised or when applied gently, is called "mercy"). God's creating the universe by the magic of his word is impressive; but that takes a back seat to his destructive energy, as in the Flood or his many other murderous interventions in human history. Thus, we have the dazzling display of omnipotence in his destruction of Sodom and Gomorrah: "Then the LORD rained upon Sodom and upon Gomorrah brimstone and fire from the LORD out of heaven. And he overthrew those cities, and all the plain, all the inhabitants of the cities, and that which grew upon the ground. ... And he (Abraham) looked towards Sodom and Gomorrah, and toward all the land of the plain, and beheld, and, lo, the smoke of the country went up as the smoke of a furnace" (Gen. 19.24-25, 28). Of course, all that was a lot more impressive back in the technological *jahiliyya* before the invention of carpet-bombing.

Yahweh puts on an equally sensational show in the Book of Exodus, when he drowns "the chariots and horsemen and all the host of Pharaoh" (14.28). Once across the Red (or Reed) Sea he defeats Amalek and his people with Joshua's sword (Ex. 7.13).He has the sons of Levi butcher 3,000 Israelite idolaters (Ex. 32.28). He has the Israelites annihilate the king of Arad and the Canaanites (Num. 21. 3-4), King Sihon and the Amorites (Num. 21.24), King Og of Bashan (Num. 21.25), the five kings of Midian (Num. 31.8), the five kings of the Amorites (Josh.10. 22-27), etc. In the early days of the kings (2 Sam. 6.7), God strikes Uzzah dead for daring to lay a naively helpful hand on the holy ark of the covenant; and he kills 70,000 Israelites with a plague after he tricks David into giving the wrong answer to the prophet Gad's riddle (2 Sam. 24. 13-15). In the New Testament such demonstrations of power drastically diminish, except for minor episodes, like the drowning of the Gadarene swine (Mk. 5.13), the zapping of Ananias and Sapphira (Acts 5), and the smiting of Herod Agrippa (Acts 12) for not giving glory to God.

On the other hand, Christian Scriptures end with a spectacular burst of predicted divine violence in the Book of Revelation, which also tackles the nagging question, Why has God left us in the lurch for so long? Heart-warming as all the scriptural accounts of fancied godly rage and glory were, they had one supreme defect: they came early on, faded away with the passage of time and never reappeared, except in liturgical memory. Whenever the "age of miracles" gets mentioned, it seems the speaker has to admit that it's over.

Once the Exile began in 586 BCE, and in fact well before then, theophanies end: God stops appearing to, and working miracles for, the people of Israel. Later historical events such as the fall of Babylon in 538 BCE and the return of some of the Jews exiled there to Judea, were credited to the Lord by pious patriots; but they could have just as easily been viewed as secular happenstance. And had they been consistent, the nationalist zealots who continued to see God's hand in everything should also have blamed YHWH for the catastrophes of the Jewish War (66-70 CE), the Crusades, and the

Holocaust; but, needless to say, only a few did. Still, at least they had their dream visions, like those in the Book of Daniel, even as Christians had theirs in Revelation. Since sacred time and salvation history had basically proved to be a bust, for example to persecuted Jews in the 2nd century BCE and to persecuted Christians in the first century CE, there was no escape except in an apocalyptic future, which might in theory dawn any day now, although it never did.

Both Christians and Muslims (moved by the near-hysterical anticipation of a bloody Judgment Day in the New Testament and the Qur'an) kept such hopes alive for centuries, while the sadder but wiser Jews, having waited in vain down through the ages for their permanently delayed Messiah, were and are more restrained in their expectations. They even joked about paying a pauper to be on the lookout for the Messiah 24/7—the salary would stink, but the job security would be fabulous. In any case, believers could hardly be satisfied with God's record in protecting his chosen ones and blasting their foes; and they willy-nilly had to settle for some vague salvific scenario or other. Abandoned beggars can't be choosers.

The God who they hoped would reappear and show his old flair for sensational rescues was clearly a wish-fulfillment figure, by turns and at once a personal protector, tribal guardian, warrior king, cosmic lord and master, and perfect Lawgiver. A divine jack of all trades, this protean character was a Creator, Restorer, Father, Judge, Lover, Conqueror, Shepherd, and so on. Christians accepted all of this and added self-immolating Redeemer and Savior.

But really, whom are they trying to kid? This God is plainly a projection of specific and local human desires. (A pastoral people needs shepherds, etc.) As the occasion requires, God can serve as a fertility doctor (Genesis 18, 25, 30, etc.), hydraulic engineer (Exodus 14), desert-dining caterer (Exodus 16.12-35, Numbers 11.7-8, 31-32), leprologist (Numbers 12, 2 Kings 5), epidemiol-ogist (Numbers 16), herpetologist (Numbers 21), donkey-whisperer (Numbers 22), urban demolitions expert (Joshua 6), cloud-seeder

(1 Kings 18.45), whale trainer (Jonah 1-3), and lion-tamer (Daniel 6). Talk about handy.

The list could be, and has been, extended to infinity; because, as the sum total of everyone's wishes, God must contain Whitmanesque multitudes. And notice how he performs all these functions out of pure favoritism, just as he chose Abraham and the Israelites *de gaieté de coeur*, for no reason at all. Such arbitrariness has one big advantage, though: if humans could deserve good treatment or, as Christians might say, if sinners could earn their own salvation, then God would owe them—and they'd have the right to complain when he failed—as he constantly does fail—to deliver.

The only reasonable conclusion to draw from God's repeated screw-ups in creating and controlling the chaotic universe is that, if one can even conceive of his existence, "he" must be as subject to mutability as any of his creations. Of course, all human statements and fantasies about God are time-bound, which explains the notorious evolution from the Old Testament's calling God "the fear of Isaac" (Gen. 31.53) to the New Testament's equating him with love (1 John 4.8). But how could God not be affected by experiencing the fourteen-plus billions of years since Creation? Even when humans read a work or see a spectacle that they know "by heart," it makes an impression on them. So, in "watching" history unfold, including the long, dull prelude before living beings emerged, God must have had some intellectual/emotional response, if only boredom. Or didn't he bother to watch, since he knew all the outcomes in advance? Poor God! (He never got to learn, to grow, to be transformed.)

Who knows? The Bible has God regretting he ever made humanity (Gen. 6.6) and hence deciding to drown it. God more than once wanted to wipe out his chosen people (Ex. 32.10; Num. 14.11-12). And then he switched his loyalty from the stiff-necked Israelites to the newly chosen Christians, or so the latter say. After which, Muslims claim God moved on from his lesser old-time prophets to his latest and best and final prophet, Muhammad. The God who doesn't change keeps on changing. In other words, God is contradiction personified.

He's universal, but	he's whimsical.
He's all-good, but	he permits evil.
He's perfect, but	everything he "makes" is imperfect.
He's all-powerful, but	he prefers not to get involved.
He's all-wise, but	he keeps his wisdom to himself.
He's infinitely beyond us, but	he wants us to love him.
He's all-loving, but	he's too shy to show it.
He's omniscient, but	completely silent.
He's One, but	he's also Three.
He's a "spirit," but	we know nothing about "spirits."
He doesn't need our worship, but	he demands it anyway.
He thinks about us all the time, but	he waited 14 billion years to create us.

There's no way to make all this add up. The more you look at him, the more God seems to be an *ad hoc* invention to save us from the kinetosis of time. Unfortunately, any being that transcended time would by definition be someone we'd have nothing in common with and couldn't begin to relate to. Hockey-playing kids in the Mite and Squirt leagues don't ever face off against the NHL.

And so it should come as no surprise that the God of theology plays a minor role in everyday religious life: Jews busy themselves with the Torah, not with its imaginary Giver. Christians profess to believe in an impossible, unimaginable Trinity, but spend almost all their time on their favorite human member of it, Jesus, and his reported sayings and doings. Muslims fixate on all the divine ipsedixits vouchsafed to Muhammad, while telling us little more about God than that he's great." Terrific, but then so are the Milky Way, the Great Barrier Reef, tigers, swallow-tailed butterflies, *De Rerum Natura*, the Piazza del Campidoglio, *The Magic Flute*, Virginia Woolf, Penelope Cruz, Dom Perignon, and so on—but, unlike Allah, all those things are real.

Theologians continuously betray the unreality of God by their inveterate use of the "spirit" metaphor in talking about their divine fixation. Whoever first came up with this idea must have been thrilled with the idea that God is "like" wind in that he's both invisible and powerful (so you can't bring him in for questioning). But there are less positive implications here, as in the Shakespearean phrases "airy nothing" and "thin air" or in the following anti-spiritual ditty …

WHOOSH

Ruách-ha-kódesh! Holy Spirit!
Adore it! Praise it! Love it! Fear it!
The Ghost, der Geist, the Breath of Air,
It whips off hats and musses hair
(for starters)—more, it blasts, it blows
(precisely where, though, no one knows).* (*John 3.8)

Well, let's go back to Genesis
where, like a hen in brooding bliss,* (*Gen. 1.2)
God's Spirit floats upon the deep
in silence (could it be asleep?).
For eons it (she?) hovers, napping,
until (look out below!) the zapping
of Eldad and Medad and Moses,* (*Num. 11.26-30)
where Moshe rabbenu proposes
that everyone (well, every guy)
deserves to get a Spirit-high.

Good luck! Turns out that's not the way
the Spirit works. Look, you can pray
all day and night until you're woozy.
No use, the Spirit's very choosy.
He lands on prophets,* "judges,"** kings,*** (*Ezek. 37. 1 **Jg. 6.34 ***1 Sam. 16.13)
and makes them do the weirdest things.
Take Samson: thanks to heaven's plan,

the Spirit made him Superman.
He'd mow down Philistines like grass
with just the jawbone of an ass.*   (*Jg. 15.15)
He'd slice thick ropes;* he'd tear a lion**   (*Jg. 15.14 **14.6)
to shreds, bare-handed, hardly tryin'.
Or Saul: one jolt of Spirit-juice,
and he'd immediately cut loose.
He'd roll buck naked on the floor
and spout out oracles galore*   (*1 Sam. 19.23-24)
He'd whack an ox, to spark the fight
against Nahash, the Ammonite.*   (*1 Sam. 1.6-7)
Hosea hit a Spirit- homer
by marrying a whore named Gomer.*   (*Hos. 1.2)
The selfsame Spirit later said
to Jeremiah, "Don't dare wed!"*   (*Jer. 16. 1-2)

Go figure. Well, in any case,
when Jesus sailed off into space,
he sent his Pneuma to this planet
to run his Church the way he ran it
(or so they claim). On Pentecost*   (*Acts 2. 1-4)
the "Holy Spirit" double-crossed
those old-school Jews and joined the team
of—yecch, oy vey—*meshumadim**   (*apostates)
(or Jews for Jesus, how they sinned!)
by sending down a mighty wind
and fire-tongues on Jesus' pals
(the Spirit doesn't deal with gals)
a mighty glossolalia, though,
alas, this gorgeous sound/light show
so far beyond all human ken,
could never be repeated: When
new tongue-talkers spread their wings,
all they produced was mutterings,
pure gibberish. But then, of course,
they babbled such garbáge perforce.
Because the Spirit wasn't there:

the Pneuma's nothing but hot air.

Oh no! Oh yes, when Jephthah,* say,   (*Judges 12.29)
or Stephen* "got" the Spirit, they   (*Acts 6.5)
were merely on a psychic roll,
which wound up taking quite a toll:
J. slew his daughter,* Jews stoned S.,**   (*Jg. 11.34-40 **Acts 7)
(and Saul's end was a horrid mess).*   (*1 Sam. 31)
Beware "en-thus-iasm"*! Why?   (*from Greek *entheos*,)
It's loco weed, a poisoned high, possessed by a god
pure craziness, the fantasy
that something sacred's churning dee-
p inside your "soul" (or guts or brain),
a breeze or gust or hurricane,
a sort of seizure—wait, that's it!
a holy epileptic fit.

If you're among the chosen few,
Look what The Spook can get for you:
a splendid shock, a solemn chill,
a bodiless-bodacious thrill.
Don't sweat the analytic stuff,
blind acquiescence is enough.
Just hug the Spirit to your heart.
Just sniff that sweet transcendent fart
(divine *afflatus*, so to speak,
empneusis is the term in Greek),
and off you sail to Neverland
to music by the Seraph Band
(all harps and counter-tenors), swathed
in puffs of unseen Spirit, bathed
in … *blague*, in nonsense, gassy fizz.
since that's just what the "Spirit" is.

Farewell, adieu, the Ghost goes poof
when godless critics ask for proof

that "Holy Spirit"'s any more
than just a faded metaphor,
a stupid category error,
investing air with holy terror,
hypostatizing pixy dust
to shape the "God" in whom we trust.
So farewell, Holy Trinity
(a zero times infinity),
white-bearded Father, sexy Son,
and Holy Ghost, the fuzzy One.,
pluperfect blather, triune tripe:
put "circumincession" in your pipe
and smoke it for a laugh or two.
That's stuff you'd never see a Jew
or self-respecting Muslim swallow
(but "God-is-one" rings just as hollow).
Yo, theo-junkies everywhere,
please call the friendly folks at D.A.R.E.
Believers all, give up The Ghost:
Your God's a vapor-trail (at most).

Apologies for that excursus; but the "airiness" of God really is crucial. The Mormons may believe that God has a physical body, but they wisely avoid talking about it, lest they get stuck in the tar baby of material divinity. (What kind of matter? What specs or dimensions? Located where?) Much better to wrap the LORD in a mysterious cloud of unknowing, to hide him in an impenetrable Witness Protection program. Otherwise, as the old Yiddish proverb has it, if God lived on earth, people would smash all his windows—which would be, if nothing else, a p.r. disaster. But best of all to wall him off from the crowd of snoopy empiricists by announcing that no factual findings of any sort would suffice to disprove his existence. Whence the flawless tautology: if God can't be touched, then he's untouchable, which leads in turn to the lead-pipe-cinch conclusion, don't waste any more of your time on him. He's just an airy nothing.

Chapter Four

Holy People

For thou [Israel] art a holy people unto the LORD thy God: the LORD thy God hath chosen thee to be a special people unto himself, above all people that are upon the face of the earth.

—Dt. 7.6

But ye [Christians] are a chosen generation, a royal priesthood, an holy nation, a peculiar people;

—1 Pet. 2.9

You [Muslims] are the noblest community ever raised up for mankind.

—Qur'an 3.110 (tr. N.J. Dawood)

If God is the greatest—and who can doubt *that*?—then it stands to reason that his "people" are too. Is it any wonder that all Scriptures praise the persons who believe in them and threaten the persons who don't? Granted, backsliders, apostates, and hypocrites often come in for scorching criticism, but look at it this way: If those who accept God's latest-finest-supreme revelations (alas, you can't accept *all* of them, because they clash with one another) *weren't* on average better than unbelievers, then what would be the point of divine revelation? The proof of the religious pudding is in the eating—and the fine moral bodies it builds.

But there's a dilemma here: touting your own righteousness disproves it, while self-accusation suggests humble virtue. Jews, it must be granted, outdo Christians and Muslims in the unsparing rigor of their auto-criticism. The bulk of Deuteronomic history (the Book of Deuteronomy through 2 Kings) and the Prophets is taken up with arraigning the Israelites/Judahites for their sins. As Amos 3.2 unforgettably puts it, "You only have I known of all the families of the earth: *therefore* I will punish you for all your iniquities." You're chosen all right—chosen for devastation.

Christianity and Islam both derive from Judaism; and they too call for repentance and humility. But, because they define themselves by their distance from the mother religion, they both spend a lot of time attacking, if not defaming, it: "For as many as are of the works of the law are under the curse ...Christ hath redeemed us from the curse of the law" (Rom. 2.10,13). That's why they call it the *Old* Testament. And Muhammad says, "Because they [the Jews] broke their covenant We laid on them Our curse and hardened their hearts ... You will ever find them [the Jews] deceitful except for a few of them" (5:13). And this abuse wasn't just verbal, as we see in the melancholy pages of Martin Gilbert's *In Ishmael's House: A History of Jews in Muslim Lands* (2010).

So belief makes you better, which explains why the New Testament Epistles call Christians "the saints," just as the Mormons do for themselves. In an inter-faith age—ecumenism does seem to have dawned in a few tolerant spots on the planet—such claims to exceptional status sound embarrassing; and educated believers often downplay them or deny them outright. But there's no dodging the self-centeredness of the monotheistic traditions. "I trusted in thee, O LORD: I said, Thou art my God" (Ps. 31.14). My God, our

God, he takes care of us, we're his people—it's the Bible's bottom line.

But we should probably view this less as mere narcissistic strutting (like nationalism, tribalism, cliquishness, etc.) than as a therapeutic response to the pain of being trapped in time. People caught up in the vortex spinning them and everything else into *le néant* naturally want to be assured that they have an in with higher-ups, something like being on the TSA's Precheck list, which lets airline travelers zip through security. As Moses said in a series of rhetorical questions,

> For what great nation is there that has a god so near to it as the LORD our God is to us, whenever we call upon him? And what great nation is there, that has statutes and ordinances so righteous as all this law …? Did any people ever hear the voice of god speaking out of the midst of the fire, as you have heard and still live? Or has any god ever attempted to go and take a nation for himself from the midst of another nation, by trials, by signs, by wonders, and by war, by a mighty hand and an outstretched arm, and by great terrors …? (Dt. 4.7-8, 33-34, RSV).

Note that Moses is urging gratitude here, not complacency. In fact, he repeatedly warns the Israelites not to take pride in their unique situation, which comes from God's gift, not their own merit. The key is that they have been *rescued* (and maintained in peace, love, and safety, if you can believe all that), not that *they* have been rescued. Christians will do the same thing with the idea of grace. "As Paul declares in Rom. 11.5-6, "So too at the present time there is a remnant [Christians], chosen by grace. But if it is by grace, it is no longer on the basis of works, otherwise grace would no longer be grace" (NRSV). So you *are* in fact better than the competition; you just can't take credit for it.

Holiness saves people from time by making them godlike. "For I am the LORD your God: ye shall therefore sanctify yourselves, and ye shall be holy; for I am holy" (Lv. 11.44). This is achieved through one form of other of the Law, e.g., by keeping the Sabbath or its equivalent (resting as God rested), and above all by doing justice (as God is reputed to do) and avoiding idolatry (which God isn't remotely tempted to engage in). And, notwithstanding Paul's rigid insistence on *sola fide*, most Christians lean toward Arminianism by assuming that a) you get to heaven by doing the right things, and b) you *can* do the right thing by taking charge of your life, squaring your shoulders, getting a grip, etc. Just follow the rules laid down by the Savior (though you'll probably want to ignore some of the more outlandish ones in the Sermon on the Mount), and he'll take care of the rest.

Of course, it's vital that one's prophet be regarded as the absolute Last Word, and not just the latest spokesman for the latest phase of divine interlocution. The followers of Moses, Jesus, or Muhammad each inflexibly affirm that *their* prophet announced all they, or any future people, needed to know, and from then on a little sound commentary would do the rest. But there's no way to reach a consensus; and, as the author of Second Timothy (4.3-4) predicted, "the time will come when they will not endure sound doctrine, but after their own lusts they shall heap to themselves teachers, having itching ears: and they shall turn away their ears from the truth, and shall be turned unto fables." The religious market, like the stock market, never rests.

Well, whether Orthodox, Conservative, or Reform; Catholic, Eastern Orthodox, or Protestant; Sunni or Shia, and all the bizarre outliers and in-betweens, the hosts of believers all find their place in some section or niche of the *qehilla*, Church, or *umma*. They're all now officially part of the Holy People. But what precisely is this enhanced status? One might call it gilt by association: a subjective (at least) shine reflecting assimilation to a living theistic entity. But the metaphor of radiance, though it has a long religious history (the pillar of fire at night in the wilderness of the Sinai, etc.), has to give way to the more ambitious organic metaphor of incorporation of believers into a vast holy Body.

This idea is most elaborately developed in Christianity; but it's present in all forms of monotheism, and has all sorts of grand implications, the grandest of which is that any living part of a divine entity is himself or herself divine. And though the assorted monotheistic clerics constantly demand selflessness of the faithful, there is no gainsaying the ontological superiority of the community's members. Thanks be to God, *they're* a holy People, and—however harsh it may seem to have to say this—other peoples are not (although some alien souls may be, unbeknownst to themselves, anonymous members of the club). And, as Paul keeps stressing, *noblesse oblige*: "Put on therefore, as the elect of God, holy and beloved, bowels of mercies, kindness, humbleness of mind [don't let your greatness go to your head], meekness, long-suffering, forbearing one another and forgiving one another, …: even as Christ forgave you, so also do ye" (Col. 12.13) Be like Christ, since you *are* like Christ. For we are jolly good fellows, which nobody can deny.

Once again, if you call this sacred condition "grace," you stress its undeserved nature (gotten gratis) and the often lackluster qualities (humanly speaking) of its recipients, but that only highlights the awesome final results. Paul to the Corinthians: "For consider your call, brethren; not many of you were wise according to worldly standards, not many were powerful, not many were of noble birth; but God chose what is foolish in the world to shame the wise, God chose what is weak in the world to shame the strong … so that no human being might boast in the presence of God. He is the source of your life in Christ, whom God made our wisdom, our righteousness and sanctification and redemption; therefore, as it is written, 'Let him who boasts, boast of the Lord'" (1 Cor. 1.26-27, 29-31, RSV).

So, in the end boast away, even though believers aren't personally responsible for their fabulous transformation. But that sounds like hairsplitting: once you've been given a gift, it's yours. Go ahead and endorse that check, deposit it, spend it, whatever. Naturally, in this case the gift is quite imaginary—but here, if anywhere, thinking makes it so. And the thought in the minds of believers is that they've been lifted to a rarified level of being, that they're now the object of God's favor and under his protective wing--perhaps somewhat as Bernie Madoff's investors thought they were in safe and fantastically profitable hands.

But doesn't this notion of being God's special people sound like just another Walter Mitty mythology, a kind of corporate auto-eroticism, popular because it serves, or can serve, as therapy for our lonely, time-bound existence? Company is comforting but how much more so when we see those familiar faces around us (which in most religious communities mirror our own racial, ethnic, social, etc. identity) radiating, however faintly, the gleam of a divine presence. Thus, the Talmud informs us that anywhere a Jew comes in, light comes in as well (Shemot Rabbah, 6), that Israel is the heart of humanity (Zohar iv, 221b), that ordinary conversation of Jews in Israel is Torah (Wayyikra Rabbah, 34, 7), and so on. In the mouths of tens of millions of Christians, past and present, the very word "Christian" is taken to mean practically every known form of excellence. In the 2012 Republican primaries many evangelicals found it hard to vote for Mitt Romney for fear he might not be a Christian. Millions of Muslims think the Mossad pulled off 9/11, because Muslims just don't do such things. And Muslim nations have always assumed that non-Muslims were essentially inferior, typically levying a special tax on them and often forcing them to wear distinctive garments. After all, didn't God himself say, "Prophet, make war on the unbelievers" (9:73); so equality was out of the question. But "kaffir" is no dirtier a word than "gentile" (*shaygetz, shiksa*) or "non-Christian" (or, still worse, "un-Christian").

As for the cult of the saints, in the sense of pre-approved candidates for eternal happy-ever-aftering, the Catholic Church has a huge lead on other religious bodies. Jews, Protestants, and Muslims have always tended to see any over-the-top veneration of mere mortals as a form of superstition, if not blasphemy; so they've generally lagged in identifying and celebrating their holy heroes. And orthodox Sunnis have long waged war against the shrines of Shia saints.

But not to worry. All believers think they enjoy, thanks to God's inscrutable wisdom and infinite power, a unique chosenness, as marked by an assortment of ceremonies and signs: baptism (and/or being born again), circumcision, confirmation, ordination, flaunting crosses on their necks or Jesus-fish on their cars, wearing tsitsit or kippot, beards or veils, fasting (on Yom Kippur and Tisha B'Av or for all of Ramadan), saying prayers, singing hymns, attending services, professing the one true faith, and, where appropriate, pitying, despising, hassling, or killing unbelievers who have missed the straight path and "straight opinion" (ortho-doxy).

As beneficiaries of this platinum-card status (having "the seal of God on their foreheads" [Rev. 9.6], and not the mark of the beast [Rev. 14.9]), believers are set free, in fancy if not in fact, from the curse of time: The past is all about the coming of the Mighty Prophet (Preparations for; Sad State of the World without; Everlasting Triumph of). The present celebrates his totally true message; and the future will reward the faithful with orgasmic bliss. And it couldn't happen to a nicer group of people.

But let's cut to the ethical chase: does religion, in general or in particular, improve (or worsen) people's behavior? Does it make them-us kinder, gentler, etc.? We know how religious believers answer this question, even as we know with statistical certainty that Americans and other primitive peoples find atheists suspicious, if not loathsome. But is there any hard evidence that the pious are more peaceable, compassionate, or helpful than the impious?

Countless factoids have been cited in this discussion, from the atheism of Joseph Stalin (an ex-seminarian) and Mao Zedong as the explanation for their regimes' atrocities to recent headlines about atheists scoring higher than Christians on morality tests (and being better informed about religion than religionists). But the larger truth appears to be that even if we could agree on what constitutes good behavior (avoiding contraception and abortion? practicing jihad? torturing terrorists? expanding West Bank settlements? veiling women?), the components of human action are so maddeningly complex that analyzing—or just naming—them all is all but impossible. How to separate and weigh the influence on behavior of a myriad genetic, sexual, psychological, historical, situational, economic, cultural, legal, and so forth factors? What if we leave out of the equation the usual naïve varieties of free will? And how to quantify the credibility of people's claims to be "adherents" of any given religion, or the downright immorality of many divinely approved religious codes (see Chapter 7, "Holy Laws")? If we followed the Torah, the New Testament, or the Qur'an to the letter, we'd still have slavery.

So there's no basis for giving any tribe, people, or nation the imaginary unctuous appellation "holy." That's simply flattering yourself and your group for the head start you have in the race to escape the prison of time (a caucus race in reverse, where all the runners lose). So holiness is, among other things, apartness, the fear of getting bogged down with others in the slough of sameness. With their characteristic legal genius, the Jews expressed this idea in the form of a contract. In Exodus 19.4-6, God bids Moses tell the Israelites: "Ye have seen what I did unto the Egyptians [your basic odious others], and how I bore you on eagles' wings [a show-stopper, if He says so Himself] and brought you unto myself. Now therefore, if ye will obey my voice indeed, and keep my covenant, then ye shall be a peculiar treasure unto me above all people: for all the earth is mine. And ye shall be unto me a kingdom of priests, and a holy nation."

This is brilliant. Scatterbrains make verbal promises; serious businessmen (and women, though they're scarce in sacred texts) draw up covenants. And this God (as befits the poets and prophets who created Him) is not some absent-minded rich uncle; he drives a hard bargain. His favor can't be earned—which would make it a merely human product—but neither does it come cheap. This deal makes both parties look good; and it's the model for all future theistic ego-trips. It may look like a bit of luck to have, like Abraham, caught God's eye in the first place; but the Lord is demanding. Paul makes a big fuss over the fact that, "Abraham believed God, and it was counted unto him for righteousness" (Rom. 4.3); in other words, that his covenant with God was sealed centuries before the giving of the Law, and so was emphatically not a fair-value exchange. But James (2.21) trumped Paul with a simple question, "Was not Abraham our father justified by works, when he had offered Isaac his son upon the altar?"

Holiness comes at a price. Even Isaac had to go through a certain amount of holy terror before being relieved by the ram caught in the thicket (n.b., a ewe would never have worked). And Jesus not only went through his holy agony and crucifixion; he also flatly insisted, in a verse not often insisted on from Christian pulpits, that, "he that taketh not his cross, and followeth after me [to a grisly death] is not worthy of me" (Mt. 10.38). O.k., o.k., believers see that as a heroic ideal, not a sine qua non requirement; but again discipleship is supposed to be expensive.

Worse yet, even if they pay all their dues, Christians are constantly enjoined to be modest about their prospects of salvation, along the lines of the classic bumper sticker, "Christians aren't perfect—just forgiven." (Forgiven for a debt a billion times their power to repay.) No wonder they feel holy, though they're constrained from saying so without careful stipulations. It's one of the main ways religion rewards its followers: the sense of purity and well-being attested to by millions of Jews, Christians, and Muslims, especially after praying, fasting, confessing sin, doing penance, donating money, going on pilgrimage, etc. Whereupon they falsely conclude that all these visceral reverberations are not only real, but somehow or other divine, Fed-Exed from on high. Such confusion is pardonable, but just as wrong as stubbing your toe on a walk through a darkened cellar and then thinking you have just communed with the Almighty Toe-Stubber.

From there it's no great leap to imagine that the ATS has spoken to you—and, *mirabile dictu*, in your language and dialect. (Note, for example, how back in 1858 the Virgin Mary graciously addressed fourteen-year-old Bernadette Soubirous in Gascon Occitan [*Que soi era immaculada concepcion*] rather than in stuffy standard French.) Needless to say, it would be a tremendous drag if the various monotheistic Holy Ones had to talk to literally everybody; so He or She limits Himself or Herself to select members of the holy people, who then spread the word to the masses, thereby rendering *them* holy too, at least insofar as they listen to the prophetic message. The bottom line, as ever, is, "For I am the LORD your God: ye shall therefore sanctify yourselves, and ye shall be holy; for I am holy" (Lev. 11.44). Ah, divine life—there's nothing to it.

Chapter Five

Holy Hero Worship

SAINT GEORGE AND THE DRAGON

The best known form of the legend of St. George and the Dragon is that made popular by the "Legenda Aurea," and translated into English by Caxton. According to this, a terrible dragon had ravaged all the country round a city of Libya, called Selena, making its lair in a marshy swamp. Its breath caused pestilence whenever it approached the town, so the people gave the monster two sheep every day to satisfy its hunger, but, when the sheep failed, a human victim was necessary and lots were drawn to determine the victim. On one occasion the lot fell to the king's little daughter. The king offered all his wealth to purchase a substitute, but the people had pledged themselves that no substitutes should be allowed, and so the maiden, dressed as a bride, was led to the marsh. There St. George chanced to ride by, and asked the maiden what she did, but she bade him leave her lest he also might perish. The good knight stayed, however, and, when the dragon appeared, St. George, making the sign of the cross, bravely attacked it and transfixed it with his lance. Then asking the maiden for her girdle (an incident in the story which may possibly have something to do with St. George's selection as patron of the Order of the Garter), he bound it round the neck of the monster, and thereupon the princess was able to lead it like a lamb. They then returned to the city, where St.

George bade the people have no fear but only be baptized, after which he cut off the dragon's head and the townsfolk were all converted. The king would have given George half his kingdom, but the saint replied that he must ride on, bidding the king meanwhile take good care of God's churches, honour the clergy, and have pity on the poor. The earliest reference to any such episode in art is probably to be found in an old Roman tombstone at Conisborough in Yorkshire, considered to belong to the first half of the twelfth century. Here the princess is depicted as already in the dragon's clutches, while an abbot stands by and blesses the rescuer.

—Catholic Encyclopedia, 1912

All God's people are holy, but some of them are (much) holier than others—whence the cult of the saints. The worst of the many downsides to God's limitless perfections is his remoteness ("totally other," etc.). Christians solved that problem by divinizing Jesus, though they had to twist the tail of Scripture to do that (e.g., Mk. 10.18: "Why callest thou me good? There is no man good, but one, God alone.") But making Jesus God could also make him seem fearsome and remote; so believers concocted the cult of the Virgin and the lesser saints, homey human intermediaries between the angry Almighty and sinful mortals. As personal friends of God, saints can put in a good word for their clients, and perform the occasional favor, such as averting certain death, relieving afflicted body parts, finding lost objects, or killing dragons.

Jews in general have avoided this sort of thing, although the rise of Hassidic "wonder-rabbis" in the 19th century suggests that at least some of them borrowed their Catholic neighbors' veneration of the saints (the great majority of whom were thaumaturgic clergymen), even as the Catholics had borrowed from the pagan cults of heroes like Asclepius and Heracles. But in a remarkable, if not unique, policy of demystification, the authors and editors of the Tanakh exposed their great men to an enfilade of unrelenting criticism, as if to quash any notion that Israel's heroes were bigger or better than figures of flesh and blood. Moses, the greatest of the prophets, had an embarrassing speech defect (Ex. 4.10) and was forced to call upon his brother Aaron (a future idolater) as his spokesman. Moses repeatedly failed at controlling his restive charges, and when he botched his assignment of bidding the rock gush water to quench the querulous people's thirst (Num. 20), God banned him from entering the Promised Land. David, the much-lionized king, is also shown to be a political thug (1 Sam. 27, etc.) and ends his career as a impotent, vengeful geezer (1 Kings 1-2). Solomon, the supposed epitome of wisdom, became an utter fool as he cozied up with the motley array of foreign gods adored by his thousand wives and concubines. And his successors on the throne of both the northern and southern kingdom were, with few exceptions, a bunch of sorry losers, not to say career criminals.

Muslims made Muhammad their ultimate saint, despite clear evidence in the Qur'an that he was a violent, vengeful, lecherous, humorless, deluded megalomaniac. Although some scholars claim there are no saints in Islam. the original Ali and Hussein would seem to qualify as super-saints; and the Shias, if not the Sunnis, have plenty of saints, most notably the Messiah-like Twelfth Imam, Muhammad ibn al-Hassan al-Mahdi, who has, alas, been in Occultation since the year 941, but who will surely knock 'em dead when he gets around to reappearing. And one could be forgiven for likening the adulation accorded the vicious Ayatollah Khomeini to the cult of, say, the recently sainted Padre Pio (1887-1968), who at least shed nobody's blood but his own.

The numbers of Jewish and Muslim holy men (their holy women are few and far between) may pale by comparison with the hosts of Christian saints cramming the Martyrologies; but, given that all tribes worship their heroes, the whole thing looks more or less inevitable. Still, as with all the other modes of holiness, this one turns out to contain less than meets the eye. The most salient examples of that would be the saints who never existed. Even the Catholic Church has had to admit that Sts. Veronica, Christopher, and Philomena, among others, were legendary; while others, like Sts. George and Nicholas, have been so encrusted with fantastic tales that no one can ever uncover their historical core. More troubling is the shaky historicity of major Bible heroes like Abraham, Isaac, Joshua, Samson, and perhaps even Moses himself. (Only the most hardboiled fundamentalists would argue that Ruth, Job, Esther, or Daniel, among many others, actually lived.)

But even granting that a solid minority of saints are made-up characters, this would still leave a troop of real, if dead, humans enrolled in one branch or other of the Grand Monotheistic Salvation Army. Problems, however, remain; and they're rooted in the fictitious nature of sainthood itself. Saints, we are asked to believe, are radically different from the rest of us, whence their haloes, their godlike emanations, their beatific radioactivity. The supreme model here is Moses (Ex. 34.33), whose face shone so brightly after his chats with YHWH that he had to wear a veil when speaking to the Israelites.

Other instances of the superhuman qualities found in at least some of the saints include their ability to fly (Ezekiel, St. Joseph of Cupertino) or at least levitate (Moses, Elijah, St. Alphonsus Liguori), their "odor of sanctity" (St. Clare, St. Casimir, St. Teresa of Ávila), their incorruptible corpses (a vast assortment, from St Agatha to St. Zita), and of course their miracles (Elisha's blinding the Syrian army, Muhammad's splitting of the moon, Pope John Paul II's curing a nun of Parkinson's disease). Saints can go for unimaginably long times without eating, sleeping, or having sex; and despite their fantastic talents they never boast or show off. Even though their DNA is 100% human, the saints are in a class by themselves. Call them demigods or godlings: like the ideal classical hero (Theseus, Achilles, Aeneas, Sarpedon, Helen), they're half-divine.

Which is the basic fallacy in their nature, since gods don't exist, and there's no escaping the human condition. The most instructive, if not spectacular, case of sanctification, the arbitrary process by which individuals get transmogrified into quasi-divinities, has to be Mariolatry. To begin with, the BVM had the luck to have lived in the very distant past, where she left only the faintest of paper trails and the vaguest sense of a flesh-and-blood personality. Knowing so little about Mary (even the meaning and etymology of her name are uncertain), Mariaphiles were free to say whatever they wanted about her. But the modern glare of publicity, now approaching its electronic ne plus ultra, has withered claims to superhuman status. Even someone who once would have been a shoo-in for canonization like Mother Teresa had to face a *feu d'enfer* from the likes of Christopher Hitchens.

In addition to her immunity from fact-checkers and critics, Mary got a further post-mortem career boost from the fact that her near-divinization met a deeply felt need: to alleviate (without radically altering) the testosterone overload of patriarchal religion., which to this day vexes Judaism and Islam more than it does Christianity. Compare the oppressive hirsuteness of rabbis and mullahs with the gentler shaved cheeks of priests and most ministers. If I may be pardoned another Goddoggerel to illustrate my point here:

MAKE-BELIEVE MARY

De Maria numquam satis.

(One can never say enough about Mary)—St. Bernard of Clairvaux
(1090-1153)

Religious drool your cup of tea?
O.k., try Mariolatry,
pluperfect Catholic balderdash,
a sort of pious pot or hash
(but—damn!—without the dizzy high

folks used to get in days gone by).
Know what's the weirdest part of it?
It's got no roots in Holy Writ
(or almost none—it's wee cartoons
turned giant Macy's Day balloons,
puffed up by clerics near and far,
who made Miryām a superstar.)

Not much to work with: Luke and Matt
call her a virgin mother*—that   (*Lk. 1.34; Mt. 1.20)
may not make too much sense to us,
but Plato and Pythagoras
had virgin births : pre-curtain rings
announcing all the wondrous things
to be achieved by unborn lads,
(but not their moms!): such crazy fads
have faded now; in any case
Maid Mary's fans grabbed "Full of grace"
and ran with it in holy glee.
Just check out this brief history:

Since people could remember when,
theism's lacked for estrogen:
a dreadful flaw—how remedied?
How balance all that talk of "seed"?
"Well, it might look a little silly,"
(folks thought), "but let's adopt this filly.
and bring her into Yahweh's stable.
We'll call it the Ephesian* fable,   (*from the Council of Ephesus, 431)
and she'll be "Theotókos"—Mother
of God, exalted miles above all other
gals—but beware of female pride:
She'll still be male-identified,
Not *too* maternal, mind you, first
we'll have to bleep that extra burst
of baby-making after Jesus.*   (*Mt. 13.55-56, Mk. 3.31-32; Lk. 8.19-20; Jn. 2.12, 7.3.5)

So—and this will really please us—
let's sweep those children out of sight.
His siblings *could* be cousins, right?
and she was celibate, a nun
who happened to have had that son.
So when you paint or sculpt her, best
to lose those thighs, deflate that chest.

And thus 'twas done, but still fell short,
her worshipers craved better sport.
They said, "She must have been conceived
without the foulness *we* received
from *our* crude parents' lustful fit."
So she became Immaculate
and we turned into filthy crud—
(till scrubbed clean with our Savior's blood)—
and we bowed down before our Queen,
"O Mary, be our go-between!
Appease the Master's well-earned curse!
Don't let him tan our hides—or worse!
We'll sing your hymns, we'll tell your beads;
remember us in all our needs!"

Well, that *Regina Coeli* shtick
(or *Maris Stella*—take your pick)
was fine; but still, for all the glor-
y, Mary's Fan Club wanted more.
So it addressed the final blot
on her escutcheon: she was not
immortal; she had died like all
us sinners. Ach, that cast a pall
across the theo-scape, which led
to this diktat: Our Mary dead?
No way! She simply "fell asleep"
(Dormition) in a sort of deep
delight. She *never* was entombed;
instead the Virgin got "assumed"

straight into heaven—what a coup!
(Amazing, though, that no one knew
about this, much less saw her fly,
a sacred comet, through the sky,
until at last she disappeared
beyond the clouds, and angels cheered
her passage through the Pearly Gates,
from whence she was (the dogma* states)   (*infallibly defined in 1950)
escorted to her starry throne,
the only human with her own
(unsullied) body there—until
the Doomsday blast, when sinful swill
like you and me will rise en masse,
to get our grades, our Fail or Pass.

But she's already graduated,
with *summa*, first in class, and rated
best, *hors concours*.—Now let's talk sense:
in fact there 's zero evidence
(as far as human eye can see)
for all this Mariolatry.
Unfazed by that, the Mary-crowd
dreams on, amidst a pinkish cloud
of scapulars and rosaries,
of gooey hymns on bended knees,
novenas, litanies, the works,
a feast for sentimental jerks.
"Celestial Mother, hear our prayers!
String-puller with The Man Upstairs,
please use that pull on our behalf!
Ask God to kill the fatted calf
for us, his starving, wretched brood—
if *you* ask, He'll be in the mood."

Mon Dieu, how infantile of them,
how puerile to clutch the hem
of Mary's skirt. It's time to send

> their dear Imaginary Friend
> a last farewell. Yes, it's been fun,
> Madonna, but we've got to run.
> Your dreamy image—it's passé.
> We need a new look for today:
> Not some sweet nothing who gets told
> her role, and then—good girl!—obeys,
> for which she wins such fulsome praise
> as Bernard's "*numquam satis*" stuff:
> that's way, way, way, beyond "enough."

Rational carping aside, it's easy to see what made the cult of Mary, like that of other holy heroes, flourish so exuberantly: the whole spectrum of good feelings it prompted and fed in its devotees, things like admiration (the heavenly Hall of Fame!) identification (s/he's one of us!), assimilation (naming children after saints!), edification (s/he brings out the best in us!), imitation (martyrdom!), inspiration (you can do it!), and so on.

But this whole routine is based on the hoary old mistake of abolishing the empirical continuum that all individuals and all things lie along, and then exalting a few specimens to a rarified ontological status. With the fading of religion in the West, people now tend to canonize media celebrities, movie stars, top athletes, centerfold lovelies, best-selling authors, rocket scientists, and, for the truly naïve, politicians (Reagan, Putin, Chávez). This fan base might not exactly imagine that their heroes, like the Olympians, eat ambrosia, drink nectar, and have ichor in their veins; but they do inhabit a higher sphere of being, don't they, if only because of all their money?

Of course, they don't; and no more do the saints. Their blessed essence resembles the eternal glory of the redeemed in heaven: the moment you try to grasp it, it crumbles like dry rot struck by a chisel. Goodness can only be defined by reference to evil. So there must be a cut-off line somewhere to separate the mostly good from the mostly bad; but where and how could it be drawn (as in "D is passing; F, you flunk")? Breaking the continuum like that would be nonsensical legalism, like the Catholic dichotomy between mortal and venial sin (an infinite number of venial sins don't add up to one mortal sin). Such thinking leads to the binary realms of heaven and hell, to which billions of moral mutts will be eternally consigned—but at that point any fair-minded person has to snort in contempt.

Or does every human summoned before the bar of Divine Justice eventually "pass" (universalism)? In that case we can all relax and throw the whole concept of holiness away as too blurry to be of any use. Virtuous behavior is whatever matches a coherent, tested, this-worldly ethical norm; calling it "holy" is just slapping a fanciful label on it. When Latino baseball players make the sign of the cross just after stepping up to the plate, does anyone seriously believe that the once-crucified Jesus will intervene in the next minute or so and cause the batter to make a hit or an out? I mean, anyone except the batters themselves, who often point their fingers to heaven after a home run, whether in gratitude to the Sky God or in memory of a dead relative. (Wouldn't Jesus, if he were somehow still out there, be caught in a bitter conflict of interest, given the presence of other self-blessing Latinos on the other team and perhaps even on the mound?)

Sainthood, then, is an empty category. In his "Reflections of Gandhi" (1949), George Orwell famously said that, "Saints should always be judged guilty until they are proved innocent"; but that was more a protest against the crimes of holy fanatics than a claim that all saints are intrinsically phony or worse. They are, in fact, more or less like the rest of us; but for religious types the merely human isn't enough. So they invent legends, clothe them with numinous glitz, and bask in the manufactured glow, as the Israelites did with Moses.

When he translated Exodus 34.29, St. Jerome's faulty Hebrew led him to describe Moses' face as "horned" (*cornuta*), rather than "radiant" (*koran*), which led to, among other things, the funny knobs bedecking the head of Michelangelo's Moses and a Swiftian joke about cuckolds. But the horns were no more factitious than the shining, and neither of them played any role in the spell the statue cast over Sigmund Freud, drawing him to spend hours in front of it at the church of San Pietro in Vincoli in Rome. Life is mysterious and tragic and comic and mind-blowing enough without having to pretend that it, or any part of it, is "holy." Haloes (from the Greek *halos*, meaning, *inter alia*, ring of light around the sun or moon) are a perfect example of airy nothings.

Chapter Six

Holy Books

For as the rain cometh down, and the snow from heaven, and returneth not thither, but watereth the earth, and maketh it bring forth and bud, that it may give seed to the sower, and bread to the eater: So shall my word be that goeth forth out of my mouth: it shall not return to me void, but it shall accomplish that which I please, and it shall prosper in the thing whereto I sent it.

—Isaiah 55.10-11

And I testify unto every man that heareth the words of the prophecy of this book, If any man shall add unto these things, God shall add unto him the plagues that are written in this book. And if any man shall take away from the words of the book of this prophecy, God shall take away his part of the book of life, and out of the holy city, and from the things which are written in this book.

—Revelation 22. 18-19

This book is not to be doubted.

—Koran 2.1, tr. N.J. Dawood

That brusque warning, "This book is not to be doubted," are the very first words of the Qur'an, after the Exordium. And they airlift us in a trice to the Neverneverland of Sacred Scripture. The flight from time is clearly and poignantly seen in the myth of the Eternal Word (which somehow existed before time, see Jn. 1.1-2). *Verba volant, scripta manent,* says the old proverb; but of course everything flies away and nothing "remains." Still, one can readily imagine a quasi-eternity for books. (Hell, even e-mails seem to have a kind of immortality.) And if written words can last, how much more the written words of God? After all, as we've always been told, God is the opposite of everything ephemeral.

The word of God would have to be something like an infallible Wikipedia. Open it up, and you've got your answer. Apart from the perfect accuracy ("thy word is a lamp unto my feet, and a light unto my path," P.s 119.105), it has guaranteed reliability ("the word of our God shall stand for ever, Is. 40.8), and unimpeachable veracity ("thy word is true from the beginning," Ps. 119.60). And if it weren't for troublemakers making a fuss over new "issues" (in vitro fertilization, gay marriage, physician-assisted suicide, cloning, animal rights, etc.), there'd never be a need for updates. Luckily we have rabbinical boards, the Magisterium, and the *ulema,* so the faithful can get a steady stream of horse's-mouth-quality dicta to live by.

Is there any more powerful and impressive rhetorical effect than the calm, masterful, that-settles-it tone of a preacher quoting a proof text? Though Jewish, Catholic, and Muslim clergy do this as well, televangelists set the standard here: waving their well-worn, leather-bound Bibles at the in-studio, on-location, or at-home audience (and, when as needed, opening and reading, rather than quoting from memory), Protestant hafizes recite the word of God with the unshakable authority of CNBC announcers reporting the day's final Dow, Nasdaq, and S. & P. numbers.

But there are serious problems with God's word (beyond Sportin' Life's reminder that it ain't necessarily so). Sacred texts are often cruel, violent, stupid, misogynistic, hectoring, and only too ready to bless—under the right circumstances—a whole spectrum of evils from rape to slavery to murder. Of course, some incredulous Bible-readers have been complaining about all that for centuries; and the same can be said about the Qur'an, although p.c. professors of Religious Studies and other academics may avoid saying it out loud. In any case, it's easy to find the peccant passages—see the Book of Joshua and "The Cow" surah passim. By contrast, it might be worthwhile to point out the long stretches of Holy Writ that are extremely boring and/or badly written.

This is no trivial point; but, unfortunately, the only way to make it is by quoting a sample text, taken not from the much-maligned Book of Leviticus—which is sometimes quite interesting—but from what is, all things considered, the most important book in the Hebrew Bible, Exodus (Chapter 37):

> [1] And Bezaleel made the ark [of] shittim wood: two cubits and a half [was] the length of it, and a cubit and a half the breadth of it, and a cubit and a half the height of it:[2] And he overlaid it with pure gold within and without, and made a crown of gold to it round about.[3] And he cast for it four rings of gold, [to be set] by the four corners of it; even two rings upon the one side of it, and two rings upon the other side of it.[4] And he made staves [of] shittim wood, and overlaid them with gold.[5] And he put the staves into the rings by the sides of the ark, to bear the ark.[6] And he made the mercy seat [of] pure gold: two cubits and a half [was] the length thereof, and one cubit and a half the breadth thereof.[7] And he made two cherubims [of] gold, beaten out of one piece made he them, on the two ends of the mercy seat;[8] One cherub on the end on this side, and another cherub on the [other] end on that side: out of the mercy seat made he the cherubims on the two ends thereof. [9]And the cherubims spread out [their] wings on high, [and] covered with their wings over the mercy seat, with their faces one to another; [even] to the

mercy seatward were the faces of the cherubims.[10] And he made the table [of] shittim wood: two cubits [was] the length thereof, and a cubit the breadth thereof, and a cubit and a half the height thereof:[11] And he overlaid it with pure gold, and made thereunto a crown of gold round about.[12] Also he made thereunto a border of an handbreadth round about; and made a crown of gold for the border thereof round about.[13] And he cast for it four rings of gold, and put the rings upon the four corners that [were] in the four feet thereof.[14] Over against the border were the rings, the places for the staves to bear the table.[15] And he made the staves [of] shittim wood, and overlaid them with gold, to bear the table.[16] And he made the vessels which [were] upon the table, his dishes, and his spoons, and his bowls, and his covers to cover withal, [of] pure gold.[17] And he made the candlestick [of] pure gold: [of] beaten work made he the candlestick; his shaft, and his branch, his bowls, his knops [capitals], and his flowers, were of the same:[18] And six branches going out of the sides thereof; three branches of the candlestick out of the one side thereof, and three branches of the candlestick out of the other side thereof:[19] Three bowls made after the fashion of almonds in one branch, a knop and a flower; and three bowls made like almonds in another branch, a knop and a flower: so throughout the six branches going out of the candlestick.[20] And in the candlestick [were] four bowls made like almonds, his knops, and his flowers:[21] And a knop under two branches of the same, and a knop under two branches of the same, and a knop under two branches of the same, according to the six branches going out of it.[22] Their knops and their branches were of the same: all of it [was] one beaten work [of] pure gold.[23] And he made his seven lamps, and his snuffers, and his snuffdishes, [of] pure gold.[24] [Of] a talent of pure gold made he it, and all the vessels thereof.[25] And he made the incense altar [of] shittim wood: the length of it [was] a cubit, and the breadth of it a cubit; [it was] foursquare; and two cubits [was] the height of it; the horns thereof were of the same.[26] And he overlaid it with pure gold, [both] the top of it, and the sides thereof round about, and the horns of it: also he made unto it a crown of gold round about.[27] And he made two rings of gold for it under the crown thereof, by the two corners of it, upon the two sides thereof, to be places for the staves to bear it withal.[28] And he made the staves [of] shittim wood, and overlaid them with gold.[29] And he made the holy anointing oil, and the pure incense of sweet spices, according to the work of the apothecary.

Had enough? Couldn't thousands, millions, tens of millions of writers (you! me!) do better than that—at least if they were free to choose the subject? Is there any meaningful sense in which such dross be called "inspired'? And what about all the rest? The endless ritual prescriptions of the Torah? The ceaseless sermonizing of the New Testament? ("Slaves, be obedient to those who are your earthly masters, with fear and trembling, in singleness of heart, as to Christ" [Eph. 6.5, RSV]; "I permit no woman to teach or to have authority over men; she is to keep silent" [1 Tim. 2.11]). Or the sadistic ravings of the Qur'an ("For the wrongdoers We have prepared a fire which will encompass them like the walls of a pavilion. When they cry out for help they shall be showered with water as hot as molten brass" [18:29]).

You call that Holy Writ? Even if one purged monotheism's sacred texts of all their horrors and howlers, there's no denying their essential failure to transcend the limitations of human speech. Worse yet, the more time rolls on, the more clearly we see that failure. The frenetic apocalypses of Isaiah, Jesus, John, and Muhammad look both crazier and more pathetic in the light of the many centuries that have passed since they were so confidently proclaimed. Anyone want to bet on the coming of the Messiah or Judgment Day—before, say, Burkina Faso wins the Winter Olympics?

The poems of Scripture, like its prose legends and semi-historical narratives, are no different, structurally, from their secular counterparts. Some of them, to be sure, are quite beautiful. But the real-world preoccupations of the Bible and the Qur'an look increasingly local and petty with the passage of time. What do we care about the now-forgotten Syro-Ephraimite war of 734 -733 BCE, which led Isaiah to utter his unremarkable prophecy (7.14) that, "a young woman shall conceive and bear a son"—later jazzed up by mistranslating "young woman" (*almah*) as "virgin" (*parthenos*) and applying the verse, for no good reason, to unrelated events seven-plus centuries later? Why should we bother with Ezekiel's prophecy (37) about the reuniting of the lost northern tribes of Israel with Judah under the rule of a Davidic king—which unfortunately never happened and never will? Is anyone truly comforted or enlightened by the pedigrees of Jesus in Matthew and Luke, or by the bad report cards issued to various churches in Asia Minor by Revelation 2 and 3? (Who *was* that so-called "Jezebel" making trouble millennia ago in Thyatira?) And, except as ancient gossip, why should we pay any attention today to the marital squabbles of Muhammad with Aishah and Hafsah (see surah 66, "Prohibition") or the Prophet's undying hatred of his uncle Abu- Lahab (surah 111, "Al-Lahab")?

As everyone but fanatics knows and admits, the various scriptural bulletins from heaven bristle with mistakes and immorality. There may not be a single factually or historically true statement in Genesis, vivid as its mythic canvases are. The story of Exodus is a fairy tale. Leviticus 11.6 notwithstanding, hares do not chew the cud. The sun did not stand still to help Joshua slaughter more Amorites. The body counts after battles in the Book of Judges are absurd. The world-census reported by Luke in 2.1 was never taken. There's no reason to believe that Jesus raised Lazarus—or himself—from the dead. Muhammad was completely mistaken when he claimed (9:30) that Jews venerate Ezra as "the son of God"; he confused Moses' sister Miriam with Mary the mother of Jesus (19:28), and so forth. Hence, modern apologists for religion—again, apart from raving fundamentalists—have withdrawn from the indefensible territory of biblical literalism and taken refuge in the ancient technique of creative fudging.

Ever since serious readers began thinking about Holy Writ, they made the disheartening discovery that, as St. Paul put it, "the letter killeth" (2 Cor. 3.6). But different texts have been cited as the most shocking, disturbing, or embarrassing: The Universal Biocide, aka the Flood, the worst fit of pique in history? God's wholly inexplicable choice of Israel as his all-time favorite nation (which he nonetheless allows to be savagely mistreated)? The "Father's" creepy plan to "save" humanity by having his "Son" crucified? The lunatic cult of Christian celibacy ("No one could learn that song except the hundred and forty-four thousand who had been redeemed from the earth. It is these who have not defiled themselves with women, for they are chaste," Rev. 14.3-4)? Allah's snore-inducing lava-flow of anathemas against unbelievers (19:83-87, etc.)? His continuous efforts to keep Muhammad's harem well-stocked (35:5)?

Actually, even today most Muslim commentators seem content to go along with literal belief in the many deranged utterances of the Qur'an ("Those that deny Our revelations We will burn in fire," 4:56). But, faced with their own cantankerous or hysterical passages, Jewish and Christian commentators have set about allegorizing, misreading, or just ignoring them. Scriptural interpreters are in theory the slaves, or at least the servants, of the texts; but they treat the "divine" words as a pharmacopoeia, a stock of wonder drugs to be prepared according their own specifications, then prescribed and administered to the sick souls of their patients.

But the bottom line is that the medicine doesn't work, except accidentally (as when Thomas Merton, wavering over his possible monastic vocation, did a bit of Augustinian bibliomancy, opened the New Testament and put his finger on Luke 1.20 ("And behold, thou shalt be silent"—referring to the months of dumbness imposed on Zechariah [Luke 1.5-25] for his lack of faith), thereby resolving the issue. There are no wonder drugs in Scripture, just ordinary chemicals, most of which whose shelf life has expired ages ago.

As in every other aspect of religion, there is no supernatural dimension to escape into. Words in the hands of skillful speakers can sing and dance and do gymnastics, but the empyrean they leap or propel us into is purely imaginary. Words are just words, time-bound, halting, sweaty, oily, dirty, endlessly used and reused signs, reflecting and suppressing the crude contents of consciousness that Nietzsche speaks so powerfully of in *The Gay Science*:

> The evolution of language and the evolution of consciousness ... go hand in hand ... our becoming conscious of our own sense-impressions, the power of fixing them and, as it were, setting them outside ourselves, has increased in the measure that the constraint grew to transmit them to others by signs. The nature of animal consciousness brings it about that the world of which we can become conscious is only a surface-and-sign-world, a world made universal and common—that everything that becomes conscious thereby becomes shallow, thin, relatively stupid, general, sign, characteristic of the herd ... (354)

Great artists, of course, can remake the crude, besmeared signs of language into lovely artifacts; but they can't transform them into anything "heavenly." The cult of words, like all cults, is essentially irrational. The notion of a holy text, along with that of holy persons, places, objects, and events, rests on the fallacy that the sacred-profane distinction reflects the deepest level of reality, whereas it's more like the difference between the American and National League or between Flemish and Dutch. Everything exists along a continuum; everything is connected to everything else. Saints and sinners, good and evil, the beautiful and the ugly, the celestial and the terrestrial, flow into one another. Dividing them into hermetically sealed units may be convenient, may at times be irresistible, but it's false.

Consider, for example, how the very words of God himself (and the holiest words of the Bible) could apply perfectly well to the most secular of contexts. "I Am Who I Am" (Ex. 3.14) is practically the same as Popeye's signature line. Jesus dramatic statement, "Take, eat, this is my body" (Mt. 26.26) could be repeated verbatim as an invitation to oral sex. Allah's command, "Seek out the enemy relentlessly. If you have suffered, they too have suffered" (4:104) was doubtless anticipated by hundreds of generals and chieftains before Muhammad and unconsciously repeated by thousands after him. Yahweh told the prophet Malachi (1.3), "I loved Jacob" (later quoted by Paul in Rom. 9.13); but the same line must have been spoken countless times, for example by Marian Ann Boris, the wife of Senator Jacob Javits. And, speaking of wives, when God told Muhammad, "You may put off any of your wives you please and take to your bed any of them you please" (33:51), his message was the same as that uttered by countless royal advisors to their polygynous lords, from the time of King David to that of King Mswati III of Swaziland, who as of 2012 had a harem of fourteen. And how many millions of proud new fathers have stolen a line from Mt. 3.7 (and 17.5; Mk. 1.11, 9.7; Lk3.22, 9.35; 2 Pet. 1.17)—or beaten the Bible to the punch—by declaring, "This is my beloved son in whom I am well pleased"—if not verbatim, then in roughly the same words. You can copyright—for 75 years or so—certain collocations of words, but the only words you can patent are brand names.

In many irreducible ways, talk is cheap. The same words in different settings mean different, often contradictory, things. "You will destroy a mighty kingdom"; Epimenides the Cretan said, "All Cretans are liars" (Titus 1.12); "Let him have it" (google "Derek Bentley"). Any sentence, however magniloquent, can be distorted or destroyed by pronouncing it in a weird tone or accent. The same dishes listed on a restaurant menu will be read with a very different eye by carnivores and vegans, just as the same election results in the newspaper evoke wildly different responses from Republicans and Democrats.

So the myth of sacred words and texts dissolves in the acid bath of serious questioning. Sacred words are ordinary words. God, in any case, never spoke any words, because only humans speak human languages. The authors of sacred texts imagined or pretended that they heard messages from Someone in the Great Beyond. In a predictable coincidence the words of the Almighty issue forth in a style closely resembling the author's, with all his (God almost never speaks on the record to women) quirks and habits. And, irritatingly enough, despite God's omniscience, he never once reveals a concrete fact about the universe or the laws of nature that humans didn't know already. What would it have cost him to at least drop a hint, back in the old days when he regularly communicated with the prophets, about heliocentrism, antisepsis, evolution, the periodic table of the elements, etc.? What would it cost him now to give us a cure for AIDS, explain the Higgs boson, or settle the disputes about life on other planets?

Ain't gonna happen. Any of that would require real transcendence, a bridge from the human sphere to the Other World; but neither the bridge nor that World exists. And the proof of this can be found in the holy books, with their holy words, that believers are forever touting. One need go no farther than YHWH's most celebrated oracle, the Ten Commandments, where he says, "I, the LORD thy God, am a jealous God, visiting the iniquity of the fathers upon the children unto the third and fourth generation of them that hate me" (Ex. 20.5).

Oh, those third and fourth generations. Human memory may have a gravitational date with oblivion, but God, his prophets insist, will go on punishing the spawn of the wicked. What actually happens is that, as Walter Kauffmann reminds us, the shifting tides of time sooner or later swamp and bury belief in the Lord of Eternity:

FADEAWAY

The master [Baal Shem Tov] used to go to a certain place in the woods and light a fire and pray when he was faced with an especially difficult task—and it was done. His successor, the so-called great Maggid, followed his example and went to the same place but said: "The fire we can no longer light, the prayer we no longer know; but we can still say the prayer"—and what he asked was done, too. Another generation passed, and Rabbi Moshe Leib of Sassov went into the woods and said: "The fire we can no longer light, and the prayer we no longer know; all we know is the place in the woods, and that will have to be enough." And it was enough. In the fourth generation, Rabbi Israel of Rishin stayed at home and said: "The fire we can no longer light, the prayer we no longer know, nor do we know the place. All we can do is tell the story. According to Agnon, the novelist from whom [Gershom] Scholem got the tale, and according to Buber, too, that proved sufficient.

They fail to add what the next generation said: "The fire we cannot light, the prayer we do not know, and the place we do not know. We can still tell the story, but we do not believe it."

—Walter Kaufmann, *Critique of Religion and Philosophy*
(1958)

Oy, devolution! Going ... gone!
The Shekhinah once brightly shone;
but now it's out, extinguished, poof.
Once everywhere, God's now aloof.
He used to like to shoot the breeze
with us; but it's been centuries
since He last spoke--unless, mayhap,
you count that Book of Mormon crap.
And the Qur'an's a boring brew
(no stories*) vis-à-vis the New   (*or very few and all dull)
Testament, itself a feeble sequel
to the Tanakh, no way its equal.

God's maiden speech was thus his best
(but was it *his*? Folks will contest
that point forever, so let's end it:
the Bible's grand, whoever "penned" it—
at least some parts, Job, Psalms, and such,
before the Author lost his touch).
Sure, go ahead, believers, frown:
religion's course is down, down, down.

It starts out with a Golden Age,
when miracles bedeck the stage:
the Red Sea split, the sun stood still,
the instant cures without a pill,
those gorgeous legends (true or not),
those Yahweh-stunts that hit the spot.
But—what a drag—it doesn't last:
The Age of Miracles shoots past
and then can never be repeated
(which leaves believers feeling cheated).

So what to do? Be loud in praise
of wonders from the olden days
(not now, alas, though some have tried,
perhaps faith's batteries have died).
Worse yet, as time goes by, the glow
from God's miraculous flambeau
goes darker: Doubts begin to cluster
"The LORD hath done this!" won't pass muster.
Lit bushes burn, dead men don't rise;
and virgin birth's one weird surprise.
Both Noah's ark and Jonah's whale
are equally beyond the pale.

So shrewd believers, faced with this,
just cry out "Symbol!" and then kiss
the sacred text—Thank God, all's cool!
The obsolete parts? They're a school

of Truth *im Werden**: Hey, things change: (*in development)
goodbye to stoning, *herem**, ange-   (*ethnic cleansing)
ls, hell, and all that sexist stuff.
The ancient ways were way too rough.

Hail, demythologized belief!
It brings such wonderful relief
from fables; yet, if truth be told,
its temperature runs rather cold.
The fire's doused, the prayer has fled;
no path to find "the place"; instead
beleaguered souls can just retell
the same old stories; but the spell
is broken; mere nostalgia can't
revive the dried-out, withered plant
of faith.*   (*cf. Jonah 4.6-7)

       But don't give up the fight,
ye semi-faith-full Sons of Light
(and Daughters too). If you can bear
to swallow such pathetic fare,
such feeble, faded memories
(who else but church mice eat that cheese?),
chow down, meanwhile we faith-less cats
(who prowl for reasons, data, stats)
will search for far more solid food
than Torah and the Holy Rood.
No secret spells, no sacred fire,
no magic stories (and no choir
of bearded *tsaddikim* * or saints   (*holy men)
to drown out logic's loud complaints):
we'll get some floodlights, maps, and gear
to cross this jungle. Never fear,
we know we won't get out alive,
but whilst exploring we can thrive—
unlike the God-hounds (it's their choice)

still howling for their Master's voice.

That voice again! (*vox et praeterea nihil*): "Where art thou?" "Abraham!" "Moses! Moses!" Wherefore hast thou smitten thy ass these three times?" "Be strong and of a good courage!" "The LORD is with thee, thou mighty man of valor!" "Samuel!" "Go up! ... Unto Hebron!" "Ask what I shall give thee." "Arise, get thee to Zarephath, which belongeth to Zidon, and dwell there." "Whom shall I send and who will go for us?" "Before I formed thee in the womb, I knew thee." "Son of man, stand upon thy feet, and I will speak unto thee." "Hail, thou that art highly favored, the Lord is with thee." "Hear ye him!" "Saul, Saul, why persecutest thou me?" "Rise, Peter, kill, and eat!" "So then because thou art lukewarm, and neither cold not hot, I will spew thee out of my mouth." "Know that We [Allah] send down to the unbelievers devils who incite them to evil" (19.83).

But enough of this, since all the holy books are crammed with reams of verbatim quotations from the Most High as dreamt up by foggy-minded visionaries, most of whose real names we'll never know (how many separate prophets wrote the Book of Isaiah?). And those *ipsissima verba* are available for free online. The Lord, it seems, is just as loquacious as his fans—or was, before he went mute in modern times. But no need to worry, the scribal types, who used to take divine dictation—from themselves—are as willing as ever to repeat and preach about their fabulous airy nothings, which never go out of style.

Chapter Seven

Holy Laws

When you buy a Hebrew slave, he shall serve six years, and in the seventh he shall go out free, for nothing. ... If his master gives him a wife and she bears him sons or daughters, the wife and her children shall be her master's and he shall go out alone. But if slave plainly says, "I love my master, my wife, and my children; I will not go out free," then His master shall bring him to God, and he shall bring him to the door or the Doorpost; and his master shall bore his ear through with an awl; and he shall serve him for life.

—Exodus 21.2, 4-6 (RSV)

Let all who are under the yoke of slavery regard their masters as worthy of all honor, so that the name of God and the teaching may not be defamed. Those who have believing masters must not be disrespectful on the ground that they are brethren rather they must serve all the better since those who benefit by their service are believers and beloved.

—1 Tim. 6.1-2 (RSV)

God makes this comparison. On the one hand there is a helpless slave, the property of his master. On the other, a man on whom We have bestowed our bounty, so that he gives of it both in

> private and in public. Are the two equal? God forbid! Most men have no knowledge.
>
> —Qur'an, 16:74

One of the least convincing passages in Plato is the scene in the *Crito* where the personified Laws appear to Socrates and explain why he has no right to run away from his impending death sentence. They tell him (50E)—and he agrees—that he is their "child" and "slave," and so he must endure his manifestly unjust verdict, since to do otherwise would be a shameful act of ingratitude and would set a terrible, subversive example. Socrates has other reasons for staying and facing the music; but this one has to be the dumbest.

Civil laws, we know, are all more or less temporary, makeshift, fallible arrangements. And any combination of laws and legal manipulation that condemned Socrates to death was worse than useless. The absurdity of sacrosanct religious law is that it pretends to have escaped these limitations and to have come down from some eternal realm of timeless truth. "The law of the LORD is perfect," intones Ps. 19.7 in a perfectly nonsensical effusion. Prove it.

First of all, what and where is "the law of the LORD"? And if it existed, how could we get our hands on it? Evidently through glorious divine oracles piped down into human time and space and voiced by the prophets. Nice idea, but it turns out that all recorded lists of such laws are bursting with folly and meanness. God's legal wisdom calls or called for ethnic cleansing, aka genocide (Dt. 7.1-6), polygyny (Dt. 21.15), liberal application of the death penalty for crimes including blasphemy (Lv. 24.16), apostasy (Dt. 13.91-10), gay sex (Lev. 20.13), juvenile delinquency (Dt. 21.20-12), and premarital loss of virginity (Dt.22.21). Judging from his regulations issued to Jews, Christians, and Muslims, God was a stalwart supporter of slavery—he said there was no penalty for beating one's slave to death, so long as the slave survived a day or two, "for the slave is the owner's property," Ex. 21.20-21,NRSV)—until some of his ultra-sensitive followers changed their minds about that. After the bizarre Mosaic code, later incarnations of divine law were to be found in the Inquisition, Roman and Spanish, the Albigensian crusade, bans on divorce and contraception, the declaration of papal infallibility, holy war, sharia, with mutilation of thieves, murder of apostates, stoning of adulteresses, humongous animal sacrifices, etc. And then there are the off-the-wall dietary rules of Judaism and Islam, which inculcate cruelty to animals, along with preposterous fears of ritual impurity and the outrageous, arrogant assumption—fully shared by Christianity—that animals were created for human pleasure and convenience. You name 'em, you own 'em.

The only reasonable response to all this is to reject "divine law" outright as an infantile, and sometimes dangerous, absurdity. How could a Lawmaker with practically nothing in common with us (disembodied, self-contained, flawless, beyond time and space as he is) know the best way to manage our affairs? How could there be any laws whose origin and function couldn't be explained by the milieu they arose in? Why do the holy laws of monotheism come smudged with a million tribal fingerprints, but nary a trace of a transcendent Author? What made God decide that it's wrong to eat adult pigs, but not baby calves? That it's essential to snip off the foreskins of little boys? That menstruation is "unclean"? That deserted Orthodox wives can't remarry without a *get*? That making test-tube babies is a sin? That evolution is an impious error? That men are more important than women? (How many spokeswomen does the Almighty have on his payroll?)

We like to surround the Law with regal trappings and holy ceremonies, with statues of Justice, high-columned temple-like courts, berobed judges enthroned in stately court rooms. (One of the things that makes Kafka's *Trial* so unsettling is the grungy buildings, stuffy corridors, and shabby rooms where it plays out, with the sloppy-shoddy juridical personnel, the cheaply pornographic law books, etc.)

But do we proclaim—and then expect to see—the majesty of the Law because it's self-evident—or because we realize just how much of it is dubious? Any system of laws is only as grand as its component parts and their actual functioning. To insist that there's a divine law in force (revealed to, not devised by, humans), with bountiful blessings for those who obey it and god-awful punishments for those who don't, may be a venerable old fiction; but it's nonetheless a fiction.

When it comes to morality, the supernatural is irrelevant—and not just because it doesn't exist. Ethics arises out of rationally scanned experience, the concrete transactions of everyday life, not fantasized accounts of life in ancient tales. The idea of judging actions by the supposed reaction to them of an invisible, superhuman Entity makes no sense, especially since we recall so many of the curses, once incandescent with rage, but now dry and dusty with age, launched at various times by the Most High against his shifting list of enemies, the Egyptians, the Amalekites, the Amorites, the Philistines, the Assyrians, the Babylonians, the Pharisees, the Romans, the Jews, infidels, Muhammad's critics, and so forth, plus the usual targets of monotheistic fury, the idolaters, adulterers, homosexuals, heretics, witches, wizards, and blasphemers. *Der Alte*, evidently, has zero tolerance for crimes that he himself could never commit, lacking the bodily wherewithal.

God has no right to say anything about ethics, first of all because his own recorded behavior has been so awful. Maker of a grossly deficient and ill-designed world, continuously harrowed by death and want, engineer of a world-annihilating Flood, and instigator of countless campaigns against hapless infidels ("The tribes of 'Ād and Thamūd were also destroyed, and so were those who dwelt at Rass, and many generations in between. To each of them We gave examples, and each of them We exterminated," Qur'an 25:39), the term that spontaneously comes to mind when describing God is "evil." Then we have his careless, absent-minded performance as a

Law-giver, with so many regulations that would have been better never issued, particularly the chimerical ones about "purity" (see Leviticus passim). All the evidence suggests that God simply lacks a proper judicial temperament.

But the larger truth, again, is that there's no holy law because, outside the fevered human imagination, there's no holy anything. Holiness is an imaginary category, incapable of demonstration, proof, or rational explanation, felt only by people trained or inclined to feel it, believed in by ditzy simpletons who mistake auto-erotic excitement for intercourse with "the divine." If sacred law transcended us, we wouldn't be able to grasp or follow it. If we can do either, that must be because it's more or less like other kinds of law, a human artifact composed of totally terrestrial words and ideas

Holy laws can be evaluated solely by measuring them against samples from other legal systems. Once this is done, sober analysis will find no specifiable "divine" quality, any more than one can find such a rarified quality in sacred scriptures, sacred music, or sacred art: it's just writing, tunes, and pictures. Readers have to find it more than a little suspicious that the Torah, like the Qur'an, is always touting itself, as in Psalm 19. 7-8: "The law of the LORD is perfect, converting the soul: the testimony of the LORD is sure, making wise the simple. The statutes of the LORD are right, rejoicing the heart; the commandment of the LORD is pure, enlightening the eyes." And if *that* doesn't convince you, recite 176 times all 176 verses of the brain-coagulating acrostic Psalm 119 on the glories of the LAW.

But, curiously enough, that Psalm, perhaps the world's most boring prayer, doesn't mention any *specific* laws or rules by way of showing just how wonderful the Law is. And no surprise there, because there are all too many parallels between the Bible's supposedly divine regulations and their garden-variety secular counterparts. The Word of God is famous for encouraging the beating of children—something that upstart countries like Sweden have dared to contradict: "Foolishness is bound in the heart of a child: But the rod of correction shall drive it far from him" (Proverbs 22.15). But the Laws of Manu beat the Bible to the punch, or the slap, by many centuries: "Sons and pupils may be beaten by way of correction." We all know about the oft-criticized Law of the Talion, "eye for eye, tooth for tooth, hand for hand, foot for foot, burning for burning, wound for wound, stripe for stripe" (Exodus 21.24-25). But the Code of Hammurabi anticipated this too, declaring (n. 200): "If a man knocks out the teeth of someone who is his equal, *his* teeth shall be knocked out." The Laws of Manu covered this as well, though in a somewhat milder way: "If a person has maimed part of another person's body, there shall be the same kind of retaliation, unless the perpetrator agrees to make compensation" (VIII, 2).

Be it Manu, Moses, or Hammurabi—or, for that matter, Sts. Benedict, Francis, and Ignatius, with *their* Holy Rules, and on down to the Marquis of Queensbury (who borrowed his from John Graham Chambers) and Chairman Mao's Little Red Book—the figure of the Mighty Male Lawgiver, mythical or historical or a mixture of both, seems to enjoy something like perennial popularity. Father knows best! Speaking of which, here's a jingling tour of God the Father's greatest legal hits, with a special focus on the unfathomable, mystery of circumcision. Despite its status as a primordial divine dictate (Gen. 17, etc.), that holy mutilation has recently been challenged in Germany, where on June 27, 2012 a court in Cologne banned it for any lad too young to give his informed consent. Jews, Muslims, and culturally sensitive liberals everywhere were aghast at the move; but the more one reflects on this and other sacrosanct "statutes," the more one has to wonder ...

Papá Lo Sabe Todo *   (**Spanish title of the TV sit-com*
                                            Father Knows Best)

With open mouth I pant, because I long for thy commandments.

—Ps. 119. 131

Commandments? Got 'em by the score!	
Relax, poor soul, and pant no more.	
Let's grab our Bibles, set the scene—	
It's Genesis, chap. seventeen.*	(*vv.9-14)
God makes a covenant with Ab-	
raham, demands that every bab-	
y boy must get his penis clipped,	
or rather, have his foreskin snipped,	
because … because … well, it's a *sign*	
to mark and seal the grand divine	
arrangement making Hebrew guys*	(*or Muslim guys)
God's junior partners, symboliz-	
ing … What? It's not exactly clear.	
Perhaps it's meant to teach the fear	
of God: "Look, kid, it's *bris* today;	
but watch your step, 'cause if you stray,	
tomorrow We'll lift up your tunic	
and redesign you as a eunuch."	
Hm, sounds unlikely; try this, then:	
Religion *is* a game for men.	
So "membership" demands a rod	
(though trimmed to suit our macho God).	
Why not a God-tattoo to show	
one's faith? A ring? A chain? A bow?	
Why not? Some *girl* might copy it	
(a *milah** can't be counterfeit),	(*Heb., circumcision)
which would pollute men's Sacred Games	
with (horrors!) menstruating dames.	

No bloody way! And foreskins too,
they and their owners are taboo.
So, when a *proper* penis squirts,
the LORD will get his just deserts,
as docked believers everywhere
regard their crotch and breathe a prayer
to Master Mohel Yahweh, who
admits the lads to his trimmed crew,
whose most sublime regalia
is ... their own genitalia.
Beards too! God loves a furry man*   (*Lev. 19.27)
like Haredim or Taliban,
unkempt and bristly as can be,
well maned with masculinity,
the prize rams in his fav'rite herd.

But how's that any more absurd
than all the other Holy Laws
barked forth from the Eternal Jaws,
the famous Six-Thirteen *mitzvot*
(about which all the rabbis gloat),
though half of them, at least, are nuts,
like sacrificing blood and guts
to soothe the anger of the Boss*   (*Lev. 7.1-10)
when He's pissed off, er, that is, cross.
The ban? (That's ethnic cleansing.) Sure!*   (*Dt. 7.1-5)
Death penalty? The perfect cure
for gay sex,* witchcraft,** blasphemy,***   (*Lev. 23.21 **Ex. 20.18 ***Lev. 24.16)
or, worst of all, idolatry.*   (*Deut. 13.1-12)

Need slaves? Hey, don't we all! Good thing
that slav'ry's fine with Heaven's king.*   (*Ex. 21.1-11, 21)
Need wives? And concubines? It's lawful!
(The LORD's best buds* all had their craw   (*Jacob, David, Solomon)
full.)
No hymen on the wedding night?
Just stone the bride to make it right!*   (*Dt. 22.13-21)

Plus crazy food-laws, called *kashrut** (*Lev. 11)
(though pigs and shrimp think they're a hoot),
Cross-dressing?* Charging interest?** (*Dt. 22.5; **Dt. 23.19)
Nyet!
No mixing fabrics!* Don't forget (*Deut. 22.11)
the menstru-laws*: they're God's solution (*Lev. 15.19-30)
to icky-sticky fem-pollution.
Then there's the "water of bitterness"* (*Num.5. 11-21)
to nail the sly adulteress
who's pregnant, but who won't confess.
And if a wife should grab the groin
of some guy who's in battle join-
ed with hubby, well, chop off her hand,* (*Dt. 5.11-12)
and maybe then she'll understand
how fervently the Lord of all
loves "those that piss against the wall."* (*1 Sam. 25.22, 34)
Passover lambs keep death at bay,* (*Ex. 12.1-13)
and scapegoats shlep your guilt away.* (*Lev. 16.20-22)
Pidyon ha-ben*'s a proven ploy (*redemption of the son, Ex. 13.13)
to keep God's dagger from your boy.

Oh luscious laws! O righteous rules!
Divinely cut and polished jewels!
No place is safe without this Torah—
just look at Sodom and Gomorrah.* (*Gen. 19.24-25)
Leviticus has remedies
for mold and mange and skin disease,* (*Lev. 13-14)
Shemot* lists many minute specs (*Book of Exodus)
(liturgomanes think nothing's sex-
ier) for all the gear and tackle
of Yahweh's gorgeous tabernacle,* (*Ex. 25-28, 35-39)
the altars, hangings, skins of goats,
the ephod and the priestly coats,
the cherubim, the holy ark,
expanded to a great theme park
by Solomon, who made it posh-

er, calling it *beit ha-miqdash*.*   (*Heb. Home of the Sanctuary)

Now back, at last, to circumcision,
revealed to Abram in a vision.
Who else but God could give to men
that gift beyond all mortal ken:
the weird idea to bare the glans
… unless it was some Semite clans?
A pagan superstition? Or
le dernier cri in cock-décor?

Who knows? It's all mysterious.
More thought would only weary us;
so hymn his praise, or simply hum
to Him whose wisdom we can't plumb.
He gives the orders we obey;
If they're obscure, well, one fine day
He'll tell us what those orders meant:
irrational, but heaven-sent.
Blind faith alone can pass this test.
Don't dare to doubt: Papá knows best!
Sit down, shut up: God runs this jail.
As Germans say, *Befehl ist Befehl*!

Orders are orders, and the godlier, the better. Except that blind obedience, once treasured by ancient Egyptian monks, members of the Light Brigade, the SS, and kamikaze pilots, has mostly gone out of style, along with omniscient Fathers. Holy laws, like everything else holy, are a childish optical illusion. No one actually saw them being decreed. Once upon a time someone told someone else who told someone else who told someone else that The Divinity deigned to inform his ignorant children that some action or other was required or forbidden—since they'd clearly never figure that out on their own.

But along with this great good news that God (the omniscient, the all-wise, etc.) has spelled out The Moral Truth once and for all, comes—sooner or later—the awareness that it's also bad news: Now all transgressions against TMT are made worse by being insults to the Lawmaker, who takes these things quite personally. Recall the fate of the unnamed "man of God" in 1 Kings 13, who infuriated the Lord by eating breakfast when he was told not to, and who got mortally mauled by a lion for his sin. And, beyond that, there's the anguish suffered by scrupulous types like St. Paul (Romans 7), who find that, try as they may, they simply can't keep the Law as they'd like to; and so are forced to live in a state of permanent trouble with Dad.

Wretchedly trapped in the same dilemma, Christians have been delighted to embrace Paul's miraculous cure: the bloody execution of Jesus that atones for all sins, past and future. But why should God care about human misbehavior? He made the defective creatures who engage in it, and he must have known they'd sin, as he admits after the Flood: "I will not again curse the ground any more for man's sake; for the imagination of man's heart is evil; from his youth; neither will I again smite any more everything living, as I have done" (Gen. 8.21). Awfully slow on the uptake, isn't he?

But, after all, what is that bothers him so much about our wicked deeds? None of them can hurt him; none can tarnish his infinite perfections or dampen his infinitely good mood. (And, by the way, why haven't theologians written about the trillion divine pleasures God gets to enjoy?) Here if anywhere, it seems that understanding = forgiveness should apply. But it doesn't, the Scriptures tell us. On the contrary, God-Allah burns up the pages of Holy Writ with furious accusations and condemnations of every conceivable sin— or rather, his spokesmen and impersonators quoted him as so fulminating. Even Jesus, like John the Baptist before him, sometimes adopted this tone, as in his roasting of the Pharisees (Mt. 23.1-33) or the cities that gave him a chilly reception (Mt. 11-24; Lk. 10.13-16). And Muhammad, as humorless as any Jewish or Christian prophet, hyperventilates with rage throughout the Qur'an. Strictly speaking, "fee-fi-fo-fum" doesn't appear in any known biblical or Qur'anic text, but you can constantly hear it rumbling in the background.

All of which was only to be expected. Hallucinatory, auto-intoxicated visionaries do their best basso profundo God imitation; then their successors and votaries, like Broadway producers reviving time-tested hits, replay the prophets' golden oldies. But the God they impersonate isn't really there; and his so-called laws are just as much a lie—though a far more elaborate and thoughtful one—than Joseph Smith's ridiculous golden plates. Unlike "Reformed Egyptian," Hebrew, Aramaic, Koine Greek, and classical Arabic are genuine languages; but sincere Scriptural impostors are nonetheless using them to fabulate to their hearts' content. "Taste and see," cries David, "that the Lord is sweet" (or "good," Ps. 34.8); and believers, sniffing the infinitely fine-spun cotton candy of theism, rush in to savor the airy nothings.

Chapter Eight

Holy Afterlife

But the true servants of God shall be well provided for, feasting on fruit and honoured in the gardens of delight. Reclining face to face upon soft couches, they shall be served with a goblet filled at a gushing fountain, white, and delicious to those who drink it. It will neither dull their sense nor befuddle them. They shall sit with bashful, dark-eyed virgins, as chaste as the sheltered eggs of ostriches.

—The Qur'an, 37:40-49, tr. N.J. Dawood

There's no way I can challenge the sacred eloquence of the Prophet (pbuh), but here's another "Goddoggerel" on the greatest mythological advance of Christians and Muslims over their Sheol-bound Jewish forebears: the dream of heaven.

GOOD HEAVENS!

O Paradise! Celestial scene!
Some puff-ball clouds, the sky serene!
Ah, sweet clichés! Eternal spring,
the balmy, breezy, bug-free thing!
Subtropical Edenic spot,
where earthly troubles are forgot,

where Yahweh-Jesus-Allah deign
to share their grand, galactic reign
and—whoopee!—one immortal crumb,
with gone-tomorrow mortal scum
like us. O rapture! Bring it on!
Hail, endless life! O death, be gone!

There are some blank spots still, we know,
in this divine scenario:
Like where it is and how it works
(and who could ever *earn* such perks?)
How *can* the hordes be housed and fed,
when God has raised the erstwhile dead?
They *will* have bodies of some kind,
as Paul emphatically defined.*   (*1 Cor. 15, 35-58)
Muhammad too insists we'll get
hot sex, cool drinks, silk robes, et cet.,
all thoroughly material,
not airy or ethereal.

So we'll need showers, toilets, food
to handle heaven's human brood.
Logistics! Traffic! Waste! Repairs!
What headaches for the Man Upstairs!
No sick days, down time, jobs or chore-
s—wait, mightn't this become a bore:
a whole eternity to kill?
I mean, what Sacred Tummler's skill
could keep the audience amused?
Look what the restless throng of Jews d-
id while old Moses chewed the fat
with God: the "Are-we-there-yet?" brat-*   (*Ex. 32)
s went berserk, worshiped calves, and worse—
God's presence couldn't stop the curse
or keep the sons of Israel
from raising every sort of hell.

So why should things be different when
God's sheep get parked in heaven's pen?
How long can folks wave palms and sing
in praise of (yawn) the MIGHTY KING?
Hurrah, hurrah, three cheers—ho-hum,
it's got to end in tedium.
A billion years of bliss, then what?
The godly glee will start to sput-
ter, hallelujahs limply flag
and heaven just become a drag.

Perhaps a day-trip, now and then,
to deepest hell, Lord Satan's den,
would solve the problem of ennui
and liven up the heavenly
routine: the same-old, same-old thing
of happy ever-after-ing.
Computers, hobbies, pets, and toys
might supplement the tepid joys
of heaven, might cheer up folks bored
with groveling before the Lord,
with sycophantic dithyrambs
baa-ed out by heaven's brainwashed lambs.

O.k., enough; the horseshit quota
is all filled up. Not one iota
of sense or reason can we see
in this celestial fantasy.
It's childish nonsense, gibberish,
and only children fress that dish,
plus all the infantile adults,
the ones in churches, mosques or cults.
You know the type, the pious fools
who see themselves as dazzling jewels,
too precious to be cast aside
(the fate of everything that's died)
but meant to shine upon display

forever in the skies—oy vey!

Forget it—what we are is dust,
not diamonds, *dust*, dirt, if you must
know—even Genesis knows *that*.* (*Gen. 3.19)
So when our little lives go splat,
like bugs on windshields, by and by
we *will* be swept up in the sky—
as dust, blown north, south, east, and west,
unconscious molecules at best;
so much for everlasting rest.

Of course, deep down, believers must know or suspect this too, which is why they strive as earnestly as atheists to postpone shuffling off this mortal coil and tasting for the first time the interminable Supper of the Lamb.

In the early years of the 18th century a (probably) French fraudster known to history as George Psalmanazar (d. 1763) created a lot of buzz and made good money posing as a native of, and expert informant on, the island of Formosa. Psalmanazar had a successful gig (his book was a bestseller), because almost no one in London knew anything about that remote spot in the Pacific; and the few who did were likely to be Jesuit missionaries, whose word no sensible Englishman would trust. Three centuries later, writers and preachers babbling about heaven are enjoying the same sort of fame (as of December 2, 2012, the # 1 bestselling paperback nonfiction book was Eben Alexander's *Proof of Heaven* [4 weeks], closely followed by #4 Todd Burpo's *Heaven is for Real* [105 weeks], with Don Piper's 2004 classic *90 Minutes in Heaven*, still a fond memory). Unlike Psalmanazar, they needn't worry that someone who's already been to the next world will put in an appearance and call them out on it.

One of the curious facts about heaven is how much less ink it's gotten than hell in Christian literature. Jesus himself may be partly to blame for this, because in one crucial Gospel text he strongly hints that hell has far more inhabitants than heaven: "Enter ye in at the strait gate: for wide is the gate and broad is the way, that leadeth to destruction, and many there be which go in thereat; Because strait is the gate and narrow is the way, which leadeth unto life, and few there be that find it" (Mt. 7.13-14; Lk. 13.24). Uh-oh.

In a way, that's unsurprising, since no human being, except the sinless Virgin Mary, *deserves* heaven; and only those washed in the Blood of the Lamb can even begin to hope for it. And, besides, hell has always seemed realer than heaven to the human imagination. Do 5% of the people who've read Dante's *Inferno* persevere through the end of the *Paradiso*? Homer's Hades (*Odyssey,* Book XI*)* is described at greater length and much more convincingly than his Olympus (*Iliad,* Book VI*).* Here in Pope's translation, is the mountain-top resort of the gods, as seen by Athena:

> Then to the palaces of heaven she sails,
> Incumbent on the wings of wafting gales;
> The seat of gods; the regions mild of peace,
> Full joy, and calm eternity of ease.
> There no rude winds presume to shake the skies,
> No rains descend, no snowy vapours rise;
> But on immortal thrones the blest repose;
> The firmament with living splendours glows.
> Hither the goddess winged the aerial way,
> Through heaven's eternal gates that blazed with day.

—VI, 47-56

Why Greece's highest mountain, at nearly 10,000 feet, should enjoy such year-round paradisiacal, precipitation-free weather is a mystery, but since the gods do banquet and sleep there, the invariably comfortable climate, though boring, would be a nice feature. But there's a refreshing honesty about Homer's account, later echoed by Epicurus and Lucretius: humans are forever barred from Olympus. Eternal bliss is absolutely alien to our nature.

Immutable happiness? Timeless satisfaction? Nectar and ambrosia with 24/7 room service? Is it any wonder that the gods and goddesses get itchy and drift off to watch the bloody pageant of human doings, and themselves take part with mortals in love affairs, wars, and conflicts of every sort? The ultimate problem vexing paradise—and one solved only in part by the houri-harems of the Qur'an—is that most of its pleasures are defined negatively, unlike-this and unlike-that, free from the thousands natural shocks that flesh is heir to, even as God is totally free from the deficiencies of time-bound creatures.

But life *is* constant change; and saying there's a magic domain without it is meaningless, akin to the claim, made but later withdrawn, by the bootlicking propagandists of Kim Sung-Il, that the Dear Leader never defecated. One might, in the spirit of harmonious cultural exchange, nod at another widely publicized North Korean claim, that Kim sank eleven holes-in-one the very first time he played golf (on a miniature course?); but there's no such thing as, nor will there ever be, a humanity without shit. At least the state taxidermists of Lenin, Stalin, Mao, and Kim never pretended that their beloved monsters were living happily ever after in some communist heaven.

But then does anyone truly believe in the afterlife? Jewish images of it are vague to the point of non-existence. Christian images are static and frigid, and Islamic fantasies too infantile for words. The much-discussed (and mocked) houris haven't been the main motivating force for Muslim suicide-bombers (what are female bombers promised?); or so one gathers from the fragmentary reports of failures who survived. Martyrs of all sorts appear to be swept on to death more by adrenaline and group fervor than by some sexy vision of eternity.

Actually, apart from schizophrenics or hyped-up fantasts, no one can *really* believe in heaven. Jesus says next to nothing about it. Paul flies off into blank verbiage: "Eye hath not seen, nor ear heard, neither have entered into the heart of man, the things which God hath prepared for them that love him" (1 Cor. 2.9). (Is it just an accident that the most famous citation of these lines comes in the asinine Bottom's mangled version of his "dream" in *A Midsummer Night's Dream*?) And it couldn't be otherwise: "heaven" is just a desperate cry in the night, a baseless hope of escaping time into permanence—except that we have no idea what permanence is and so can't really imagine it.

One not-too-promising glimpse of human permanence has been provided recently by a South Korean firm that turns the powder from cremated bodies into shiny little beads, mostly white, but with an occasional black, gray, blue, and green tinge (www.latimes.com/ …/la-fg-south-korea-death-beads-20120122,0,268 …).While much more durable than rotting flesh, crumbling bones, or volatile ashes, and far more esthetically appealing than such stuff, the beads don't come close to what we think of as life. In fact, when images of living forever arise, the most vivid —and horrific—of all may be Swift's struldbruggs, whose wrinkled faces and disgusting bodies—unlike the heavenly *putti*—can actually be seen, by the millions, in hospitals, nursing homes, and assisted living warehouses across the land.

Of all the dreams, delusions, and downright lies professed by religion, the nonsense of life after death has to rank as the most pathetic and childish. Without the flimsiest shred of evidence or faintest ground of hope, clergy and pious laity prate about everlasting life, because once upon a time their benighted ancestors had a revelation, somehow, somewhere, that their precious selves, their best beloved and all like-minded people would marinate in bliss after death (even while their enemies fried forever). Closure!

The invention of heaven was the ultimate twofer: it answered the otherwise dumbfounding question of why the world shows so few signs of maintenance by the kindly Father who created it; and it offered therapy for everyone's worst fear. For the first, there was no denying that the world *looked* unredeemed. It *looked* as if crime paid, injustice triumphed, and the wicked prospered—consider, macrocosmically, the history of warfare or, microcosmically, the judicial murder of Jesus (minus the hokey part about the resurrection). The front page of every newspaper shows who's in charge of the world, and it ain't Yahweh. But Judgment Day, though it wouldn't be the do-over earth desperately needs, might well satisfy the broken hearts and spirits of the billions who believe they got a raw deal whilst trudging through the aptly named vale of tears.

But then in fact it wouldn't. The whole idea of a time-stopping, binary (saved/damned) Grand Finale, is so ludicrous that it falls to pieces the moment you pick it up. An infinite reward (or sentence) for a finite performance? Do we get report cards? A diploma? Is there an appeals process? Since God must logically be at least as benevolent as your run-of-the-mill utilitarian, mustn't he too want the greatest happiness of the greatest number? And if so, how could he ever stop time and thereby end one of its key functions: the generation of new candidates for the kingdom of heaven? Who would ever want to put a limit on the number of souls packed into the bleachers for the Beatific Vision? Plus, once the lucky few or many get there, they spend eternity doing *what*? Unbelievable.

And because such scenarios can't be believed, they can't console. There isn't even any solid evidence that deceiving oneself about an afterlife makes living or dying here and now any more bearable. And why should it? Potemkin villages can't be lived in; the most you can do is barely make them out as they roll by in the dim distance. Fittingly enough, the story about the Catherine the Great and the Potemkin Villages is itself a fiction; and so *a fortiori* are all the tales about the Celestial Village, built by countless generations of God-drunk architects and carpenters. Now and forever, nothing will come of nothing.

Conclusion

The Triumph of Time

Remember now thy grave in the days of thy youth, while the evil days come not, nor the years draw nigh, when thou shalt say, I have no pleasure in them; While the sun, or the light, or the moon, or the stars, be not darkened, nor the clouds return after the rain: In the day when the keepers of the house shall tremble, and the strong men shall bow themselves; and the grinders cease because they are few, and those that look out of he windows be darkened, And the doors shall be shut in the streets, when the sound of the grinding is low, and he shall rise up at the voice of the bird, and the daughters of music shall be brought low. Also when they shall be afraid of that which is high, and fears shall be in the way, and the almond tree shall flourish, and the grasshopper shall be a burden, and desire shall fail: because man goeth to his long home, and the mourners go about the streets: Or even the silver cord be loosed, or the golden bowl be broken, or the pitcher be broken at the fountain, or the wheel broken at the cistern. Then shall the dust return to the earth as it was: and the spirit shall return unto God who gave it. Vanity of vanities, saith the preacher; all is vanity.

—Ecclesiastes 12.1-8

Yes, I know, all the translations of the first verse say "Remember your *Creator*"; but the word for "creator" (*boreh*) is very close to the word "grave" *(bor)*, which makes much better sense here; so they may well have been some scribal censorship. And, as for the spirit "returning to God," that simply means one's lease on life running out. Ecclesiastes is notorious for insisting (3.19-20) that after death humans and animals go "unto one place; all are of the dust, and all turn to dust again." So what good would remembering your Creator do when you're just about to disappear forever and that pretend-Creator isn't going to lift a finger to help you?

Ecclesiastes or Qoheleth (the one who gathers an assembly), the joker in the Bible's deck, reminds us yet again why the monotheistic project doesn't work. This enormous, arresting, erstwhile hard-wired collection of myths, legends, poems, ceremonies, stories, laws, customs, traditions, buildings, letters, speeches, sermons, prayers, pictures-and-accounts and so forth constitutes a world, a parallel universe where, if, if you're gullible enough, you can settle down for good. Monotheism is a kind of mental hospital where patients with a real disease (temporality) get a fake cure (transcendence).

The Bible, and, less eloquently, the Qur'an, highlights the woefulness of the human condition, for example, in Job's anguished—and failed—attempt to make Yahweh acknowledge just how hard life is:

> Man that is born of a woman is of few days, and full of trouble. He cometh forth like a flower, and is cut down: he fleeth also as a shadow, and continueth not. And dost thou open thy eyes upon such a one, and bringest me into judgment with thee? Who can being a clean thing out of an unclean? Not one. Seeing his days are determined, the number of his months are with thee, thou hast appointed his bounds that he cannot pass. Turn from him that he may rest, till he shall accomplish, as a hireling, his day. For there is hope of a tree, if it be cut down, that it will sprout again, and that the tender branch thereof will not cease. Though

the root thereof wax old in the earth, and the stock thereof die in the ground: yet through the scent of water it will bud, and bring forth boughs like a plant. But man dieth and wasteth away: yea, man giveth up the ghost, and where is he? As the waters fail from the sea, and the flood decayeth and drieth up: so man lieth down, and riseth not: till the heavens be no more, they shall not awake, nor be raised out of their sleep.

—14.1-12

This bitter honesty certainly puts the New Testament and Qur'anic scenarios of the afterlife to shame. But Job's *J'accuse*, though it carves out some dramatic public space for free speech, leaves unchanged the absurd imbalance of power between Job and God, who never even bothers to answer Job's questions or explain what went wrong. Job should have taken his wife's advice and cursed God; that way at least he would have come out of the whole ordeal with some of his dignity intact.

In the lame *Deus ex machina* ending Job "gets back" the same number of children he "lost" (murdered by Satan) and in the same gender proportion, seven boys to three girls. We never learn, of course, who their mother was (mothers were?), nor how old Job was when he finally restocked the family manse with replacement-kids. But Job died, "being old and full of years" (aged 140, or twenty years older than Moses), which is as good as it gets in the heavenless Hebrew Bible.

Actually, the story of Job can aptly serve as an unfond farewell to the make-believe mystery of God, since, as often happens, a purported defense of the Almighty backfires and reveals his lethal weaknesses:

THE GHOST IN THE WITNESS CHAIR

Who is this that darkeneth counsel by words without knowledge? Gird up now thy loins like a man; for I will demand of thee, and answer thou me.

—Job 38. 2-3

> The Book of Job, that strange affair,
> concludes with Yahweh's questionnaire.
> First, God and Satan close a deal:
> They'll torture Job and make him feel
> the most exquisite sorts of pain:
> his wealth destroyed, his children slain,
> his skin all leprous, mind distraught—
> a monstrous fate, and all for naught,
> since Job had never sinned, not *ever*
> (a paradox that God thought clever).
>
> Job does complain to those three clods,
> his "comforters," then—duck!—comes God's
> barrage of questions, but not one
> with answers (holy sado-fun).
> But now let humans have their say,
> since turnabout is—duh—fair play.
> It may give pious souls a shock,
> but let's put Yahweh in the dock:
> "You made this world you boast so much
> about, *n'est-ce pas*? So, why's it such
> a bloody mess, in tooth and claw?
> To make us quake with holy awe?
> And why those fourteen billion years
> before the "naked ape" appears,
> the only beast to say its prayers?
> Do sharks or snakes or polar bears?
> Do bugs or germs or tumbleweed
> pay El Shaddai the slightest heed?
> And what about the endless void(s)

of gas and dust and asteroids,
but mostly nada? What's the point?
You say you run this giant joint?
Mid all that space what's earth? A dot?
A crazy play without a plot,
where life forms sprout, then rot and die?
(They're gone before you blink your eye):
T-Rex or Caesar, what's the diff?
They dance their jig, then zap! They're stiff.

And you did *what* to recompense
the dead, to make this show make sense?
Why'd you devise this entropy,
this garbage dump called history,
Those generations bound for slaughter?
Aren't they your precious children (sorta)?
Or maybe you just *like* to kill?
Does each extinction have its thrill?
That's it! So now our Q & A
is done—if you'll just nod o.k.,
Your Majesty. Your Majesty? My Lord?
Could he be sleeping? Was he floored
by Job's objections? Tug his sleeve.
No? Poke his ribs? … Huh? I believe
he must be … Help! Wait, slap his head.
He's non-responsive? Yipes, he's dead.

Well, that explains a lot of things:
his silence first of all, the "slings
and arrows of outrageous," et
cet., plus "the fever and the fret"
that Keats bemoaned: It's all because
there's no Lawgiver, and no Laws.
Necessity's the only boss,
blind, deaf, and dumb; so you can toss
that question-book. Instead,
try science, reason, use your head.
The answers given may appall

> (but then Job's LORD gave none at all).
> His righteous bluster was a stunt,
> his arrogance a hollow front.
>
> The crucial question for Our Father
> is, "Why the devil did we bother
> with absent you?" Best not ask why,
> and better silence than a lie.
> In worlds produced by randomness,
> the question "Why?" is meaningless.

What God has to offer the patriarchs—the matriarchs just get babies—is long life, prosperity, fame, and a quiet death. That's all very well; in fact it's quite fine, but couldn't you wind up with the exact same results by combining good genes and good luck? On the other hand, God doesn't ask much of his chosen lads, except for trust in him, until the giving of the Law. Thereafter, being a proper Israelite or Jew becomes an all-consuming job. *S'z shver tsu zein a yid.*

Still, Moses insists that all those mitzvot *are* doable (Dt. 30.14), and repeatedly invokes the so-called Deuteronomic principle: "If thou shalt hearken diligently unto the voice of the LORD thy God, to observe and to do all his commandment which I command thee this day, that the LORD thy God will set thee on high above all nations of the earth. And all these blessings shall come on thee, and overtake thee ...But it shall come to pass, if thou wilt not hearken unto the voice of the LORD thy God, to observe to do all his commandments and his statutes which I command thee this day, that all these curses shall come upon thee, overtake thee" (Dt. 28.1-2, 15). Sounds fair, but it's a sign of future trouble that the blessings here are summed up in eleven verses, whereas the curses take up forty-three.

In any case, the whole thing is a fraud. Moses is speaking to Israel as a whole; and we can't accept the notion of an all-encompassing national or corporate guilt. (Among other things it can lead to poisonous canards like Mt. 27.25, "Then answered *all the people*, and said, 'His blood be on us, and on our children.'") Corporate guilt was a lousy explanation for the pulverizing of Sodom and Gomorrah and the destruction of both the northern (722 BCE) and southern (586 BCE) kingdoms. But it's still lousier as a way of understanding an individual's destiny, as Jeremiah (12.1-4) noticed and complained about, "Wherefore doth the way of the wicked prosper?" etc.

And if ever there was an even faintly credible argument that good behavior guarantees the good life, and bad behavior guarantees the slammer, all that was swept away forever by the Holocaust, the God of Israel's most spectacular failure and the end of so-called sacred history. Then too, the God of the Christians and the God of the Muslims, who may or may not be the same person as YHWH, hasn't proved much better at protecting his friends and punishing his foes. Do the math.

Which is why prophets and God-talkers had to concoct the fantasy of the Afterlife—and we've already seen what *that's* worth. "Religious belief" said David Hume in *An Enquiry Concerning Human Understanding* (1748), "is a form of make-believe which ... leads by degrees to dissimulation, fraud, and falsehood." Religionists pretend that they and their customers can escape from the prison of time. They think that whatever seems to fade and fail—our bodies, our consciousness, our deepest human connections--can be rescued and preserved "forever," though they haven't the slightest idea what "forever" would be like.

They take the harshest certainty we have, the irreversibility of death, and wish it away. They take hearsay evidence that would never be allowed in court—rumors they read about people who claimed to have heard about a dead man later seen alive—and base their lives on it, or at least they say they do. And, speaking of the dead, the faith-peddlers likewise tell us that the dead are all coming back, every last one of them, even though not a single person has pulled that off before. The God who couldn't prevent the murder of 200 million or so people in the slaughters and genocides of the 20th century will somehow track down their shattered-scattered-splattered body parts, stick them all together, and breathe life into them. The central fallacy of thinkers who say things like that is postulating a holy dimension, where miracles are the coin of the realm, floating above and beyond our pedestrian reality, otherwise known as the profane (literally "outside the temple"). But temples are purely human buildings, and the eternal temple "not made by hands" (2 Cor. 5.1) that St. Paul (a world-class holy man) dreamed about was a contradiction in terms.

People make temples, and they can unmake or defile them, just as they can reconstruct and reconsecrate them (Happy Hanukkah, everyone!). They can also fall in love with the "work of their own hands" (which includes two supreme haters of idol-worship, Yahweh and Allah, two giant idols who wanted the worship all to themselves), just as they can surround their holy fantasies with elaborate creeds, codes, and cults. At the same time, however, there have always been a minority of sober critics who could see through this gaudy mumbo-jumbo, people like Epicurus, Lucretius, Montaigne, Hume, Nietzsche, or, to go back farther, Xenophanes of Colophon (c. 570-c. 475 BCE), who famously observed that if horses and cows and lions had the manual skills, the gods *they* painted or sculpted would look like … horses, cows, or lions. Bingo.

We can't transcend our nature, or write back to the Mother Nature for a radically different set of genes. We can't erase an instinctively teleological way of thinking that projects the purposefulness of human activities back into the universe. In "Is God an Accident?" (2005) Yale's Paul Bloom points to this ingrained habit: four-year-olds tell researchers that lions were designed to be put into zoos. In the same vein, an apparent majority of American grown-ups swear that, "Everything happens for a reason," i.e., a divinely ordained and almost certainly benign reason, even though they might not be able to tell you what that was.

But we can resist our hard-wired impulse to suppose bushes to be bears (extinct in the wild for centuries, when Shakespeare's Theseus first gave his speech), which leads to the various category errors this book has been mocking, above all the denial of the continuum of existence by imagining all sorts of discreet special states and magical domains that we call "holy." This is all part of psychological pattern that Nietzsche points to in *The Gay Science*, 112: "We operate with all sorts of things that don't exist, with lines, surfaces, bodies, atoms, divisible times, divisible spaces—how should explanation even be possible when we begin by making everything an image, an image of ourselves!" And there's surely no more dramatic example of this than religion.

We can't eradicate our tendency to do this, but we can become aware and mistrustful of it, like an alcoholic at an open bar. Holiness is plainly an intoxicant, manufactured and consumed for its psychotropic "benefits." As Baudelaire said,

GET DRUNK

> One must be always drunk.
> That's the whole point:
> it's the only thing that matters.
> So as not to feel
> the horrid burden of Time
> that crushes your shoulders
> and thrusts you toward the earth,
> You must get drunk relentlessly.
> But with what?
> With wine, poetry, or virtue, as you wish.
> But get drunk.

Translate "virtue" as "religion," and you have the case in a nutshell. From the standpoint of Baudelaire's "martyred slaves of Time," it's easy to see religion's analgesic appeal. But once you know that it's an opiate, and you realize how dangerous it is to take opiates while driving or doing *anything* important (like thinking) you'll want to avoid the stuff, except for the occasional recreational rush. A diet of airy nothings can only lead to philosophical starvation.